Toddler Discipline

A Simple Guide to Parenting Your Children Using Positive Discipline the Montessori Way and Sleep Training for Toddlers

© Copyright 2020

This document is geared towards providing exact and reliable information regarding the topic and issue covered. The publication is sold with the idea that the publisher is not required to render accounting, officially permitted, or otherwise, qualified services. If advice is necessary, legal or professional, a practiced individual in the profession should be ordered.

From a Declaration of Principles accepted and approved equally by a Committee of the American Bar Association and a Committee of Publishers and Associations.

In no way is it legal to reproduce, duplicate, or transmit any part of this document in either electronic means or in printed format. Recording of this publication is strictly prohibited and any storage of this document is not allowed unless with written permission from the publisher. All rights reserved.

The information provided is stated to be truthful and consistent, in that any liability, in terms of inattention or otherwise, by any usage or abuse of any policies, processes, or directions contained within is the solitary and utter responsibility of the recipient reader. Under no circumstances will any legal responsibility or blame be held against the publisher for any reparation, damages, or monetary loss due to the information herein, either directly or indirectly.

Respective authors own all copyrights not held by the publisher.

The information herein is offered for informational purposes solely, and is universal as so. The presentation of the information is without contract or any guarantee assurance.

The trademarks used are without any consent, and the publication of the trademark is without permission or backing by the trademark owner. All trademarks and brands within this book are for clarifying purposes only and are the owned by the owners themselves, not affiliated with this document.

Contents

PART 1: MONTESSORI TODDLER DISCIPLINE 1
INTRODUCTION 2
CHAPTER 1: THE HISTORY OF MONTESSORI EDUCATION 3
    How Maria Montessori Changed Education 4
    Brief History of the Montessori Method of Education 5
    Three Components of the Montessori Education Method 7
    Real-Life Stories of the Montessori System and Components 9
CHAPTER 2: MONTESSORI PRINCIPLES AND ACTIVITIES 12
    Principle: "Teacher Ways and Child Ways" or The Respect
    Principle 13
    Principle: Order in Environment and Mind 16
    Remaining Principles 20
CHAPTER 3: CHANGING YOUR PERCEPTION 22
    Quick Insight Into Brain Development from 1 to 3 Years
    of Age 23
    Understanding a Child's Perspective on Life 24
    A Few Specific Things That Impact Your Child Directly 25
CHAPTER 4: OBSERVING YOUR CHILD 31
    The Instruction Manual Every Parent Dreams Of 32
    Understanding Schemas and Sensitive Moods 33
    Eight Stages of Observation 34

CHAPTER 5: SETTING UP YOUR MONTESSORI HOME 40
  ROOM BY ROOM MONTESSORI STYLE 42
CHAPTER 6: COORDINATION AND SENSORY ACTIVITIES 47
  COORDINATION AND SENSORY IN MONTESSORI 47
CHAPTER 7: HELPING AROUND THE HOUSE 58
  WHAT CAN YOUR CHILD ACTUALLY DO? 59
  HOW ARE "CHORES" A PART OF YOUR CHILD'S MONTESSORI
  EXPERIENCE? 62
  SHOW, SHOW, SHOW, THEN OBSERVE, AND ALWAYS INVOLVE 63
CHAPTER 8: MUSIC, MOVEMENT, AND MONTESSORI 65
  WHAT CHILDREN LEARN FROM MUSIC AND MOVEMENT 66
  WHEN DID MUSIC BECOME PART OF THE MONTESSORI MODEL? 67
  HOW TO BRING MUSIC INTO YOUR HOME 68
  GET TODDLERS MOVING AND GROOVING WITH THESE MONTESSORI
  MUSIC AND DANCE ACTIVITIES 70
  MUSICIANS FROM MONTESSORI TEACHING 72
CHAPTER 9: LEARNING NEW SKILLS THE MONTESSORI WAY 74
  CHALLENGES MONTESSORI PARENTS AND TEACHERS HAVE ADJUSTING
  TO NEW SKILL DEVELOPMENT METHODS 75
  LANGUAGE AND SPEECH SKILLS 75
  NUMBER SKILLS AND CONCEPT DEVELOPMENT 77
  DEVELOPING WRITING SKILLS 78
**CHAPTER 10: INTERESTING ARTS AND CRAFTS FOR CREATIVE
TODDLER** 81
  ARTS AND CRAFTS BUILD IMAGINATION AND MORE 82
**CHAPTER 11: POSITIVE DISCIPLINE IN THE MONTESSORI
HOME** 89
  BE PROACTIVE - THE FOUNDATION FOR POSITIVE DISCIPLINE 90
  WHAT IS SELF-DISCIPLINE? 92
  ELEMENTS OF POSITIVE DISCIPLINE 94
  WHAT HAPPENS WHEN CHILDREN BREAK THE RULES? 94
  BITING, SCRATCHING, HAIR PULLING, AND OTHER PHYSICAL
  ATTACKS 95
  REGARDING SHARING 96
  SPECIAL NOTE FOR THE PARENTS 97

CHAPTER 12: GROWING MONTESSORI 98
   Key Times in Physical Development Happen in the Early
   Years 99
   Growing Up Challenges 100
   Toys that Grow with Them 101
   Parenting Habits Change and Adapt 103

CONCLUSION 107

PART 2: TODDLER SLEEP TRAINING 108

INTRODUCTION 109

CHAPTER 1: THE NON-SLEEPY TODDLER: A CAUSE FOR CONCERN? 111
   Sleep Regression and What to Expect When It Happens 112
   Signs that Your Toddler is Sleep Deprived 115
   When Should You Seek Medical Advice? 116

CHAPTER 2: UNDERSTANDING TODDLER SLEEP 118
   How Much Sleep Does Your Baby/Toddler/Child Need? 119
   Stages of Sleep 122
   Factors that Disrupt a Toddler's Sleep 125
   Other Potential Effects 130

CHAPTER 3: SLEEP ASSOCIATIONS 131
   Negative Sleep Associations 132
   Positive Sleep Associations Defined and How to Introduce
   Them 138

CHAPTER 4: NIGHT FEEDING 141
   When Should You Stop Night Feeding? 142
   Effective Tips to Stop Night Feeding 143
   Is it Necessary to Wean your Toddler from Night Feeding? 148

CHAPTER 5: THE CO-SLEEPING TODDLER: TO ENCOURAGE OR PROHIBIT? 149
   The Proven Benefits of Co-sleeping 151
   Do's and Don'ts for Safe Co-Sleeping 154

CHAPTER 6: MANAGING NIGHTTIME FEARS 161
   Stages of Sleep and How They Relate to Nighttime Fears 163
   Causes of Nighttime Fears 164

- How to Deal with Nighttime Fears in Toddlers 165
- When Should You Contact a Doctor? 169

CHAPTER 7: NIGHTMARES AND BEDWETTING 171
- Nightmares in Toddlers Defined 171
- What Makes Nightmares Different from Night Terrors? 172
- Common Causes of Nightmares in Toddlers 173
- Dealing with Nightmares in Toddlers 175
- How to Avoid Bedwetting 179

CHAPTER 8: SLEEPWALKING AND SLEEP TALKING 181
- What Should You Know About Sleepwalking in Kids? 182
- How to Deal with Sleepwalking in Toddlers and Kids 184
- When to Seek Medical Help 187
- What Do You Need to Know About Sleep Talking? 189
- What Can You Do About Sleep Talking? 190

CHAPTER 9: SETTING A SLEEP SCHEDULE 192
- When Should You Start Setting Up a Sleep Schedule? 193
- What is the Ideal Sleep Schedule for Toddlers? 193
- Effective Tips for Setting Up a Sleep Schedule for Toddlers 194
- Mistakes to Avoid When Setting a Sleep Schedule for your Toddler 199

CHAPTER 10: THE GROWING TODDLER: DEALING WITH CHANGE 203
- Making Adjustments on Various Sleeping Routines and Habits 204
- One- to Two-year-old Routines 205
- Transitioning to a New and Big Bed 206
- Dealing with Sudden Changes in a Preschooler's Sleep Schedule 210

CONCLUSION 213
HERE'S ANOTHER BOOK BY MERYL KAUFMAN THAT YOU MIGHT LIKE 214
REFERENCES 215

Part 1: Montessori Toddler Discipline

The Ultimate Guide to Parenting Your Children Using Positive Discipline the Montessori Way, Including Examples of Activities that Foster Creative Thinking

Introduction

Maria Montessori forever changed education when she acknowledged that children, particularly young children, might do best with less adult interference. She pushed against the norms of the time, suggesting positive discipline, fostering creativity, and encouraging independence from a very young age. Now, you can take her teachings and bring them into your home. You need not enroll your toddler in a Montessori school to get a head start with your child. Learn what it means to observe, build independence, and support your child through positive discipline methods.

Throughout this book, we'll explore what parents report as successful, and others report as not so thrilling. There are a variety of activities in nearly every chapter and a thorough explanation of the rich history and thoughtful development of each aspect of the Montessori environment.

Learn what it takes to get started and to grow Montessori skills with your child. Have all of your questions regarding using the Montessori Method with toddlers answered right here. You'll discover activities you can do today and identify opportunities to help your child engage and grow into a wonderful person.

Chapter 1: The History of Montessori Education

For most parents of toddlers, Montessori seems like an out of reach abstract concept that many teachers have very strong opinions about. Maria Montessori changed education dramatically, and when she developed this particular form of education, it raised a lot of questions. The Montessori method challenges a lot of traditional systems and techniques, even the methods used in schools today.

So, what is the difference between Montessori education and standard or traditional education? Italian physician Maria Montessori developed Montessori education. It is a child-centric approach to education that uses the foundation of the scientific method. It calls upon observation, hypotheses, experimentation, and conclusions. The Montessori method has been around for over 100 years.

With anything this revolutionary, there are a lot of questions, concerns, and misconceptions. Throughout this book, you'll have the opportunity to grasp the three components of Montessori teaching, Montessori discipline, the foundation of the Montessori method, and more. We dive deep into different elements that commonly appear in early childhood Montessori classrooms, and ways that parents have adopted the Montessori method for their home.

Here is a short history and easy introduction into Montessori and what to expect by bringing Montessori teachings into your home.

How Maria Montessori Changed Education

Born on August 31, 1870, Maria Montessori broke down educational barriers early in life. At 13, she entered an all-boys school and quickly excelled in science and mathematics. Much of Montessori's childhood has become legend. Maria Montessori is widely known and acknowledged as the first woman to graduate from medical school in Italy. However, Italy's first female physician was actually Dorotea Bucca. Montessori followed shortly after and was unfazed not to become the first female physician as she quickly identified that the position wasn't for her.

In 1896, she changed the course of her career by returning to the University of Rome to learn about psychology and philosophy and apply that knowledge to teaching children. Then, working as a child psychiatrist, she developed her craft and her understanding of childhood development.

Throughout her lifetime, Maria Montessori worked as a professor of anthropology at the University of Rome. She opened her own school in Rome, schools around the world, and drastically changed how educators and psychiatrists treated and worked with children. It was an eventful life, and she was nominated for the Nobel Peace Prize three years in a row proceeding her death. These nominations happened in 1949, 1950, and 1951. Maria Montessori died in Holland in 1952.

Brief History of the Montessori Method of Education

We briefly covered Maria Montessori's history as a person, but the Montessori method of education has a much more intricate timeline. In the years leading to 1906, Maria Montessori used her experience and education as a physician, psychologist, and philosopher to research and work directly with children with disabilities. She quickly identified that the needs of children with disabilities and the needs of children were much the same. They were also much unacknowledged in traditional childhood education. So, in 1906, Dr. Montessori opened Casa Dei Bambini or "Children's House."

The purpose of the Children's House was to provide education among 60 underprivileged children; all were Italian, all were underprivileged, and all showed an amazing response to the materials provided in the Children's House. Doctor Montessori used methods of scientific observation and identified that children were not only capable of deep concentration but often entered into states of peace and calm rather than outbursts and tantrums. After a few years of observation, Montessori acknowledged publicly that when given the proper environment, you can discover and provoke a child's true nature. Doctor Montessori used the term *normalization* to describe this change.

During the Children's House's early years, Montessori simply observed. She sat still and watched how the children played and interacted together. As she observed, she saw where different children excelled, and some struggled. With age-groupings larger than you would find in a traditional class, the older students tended to the younger. Children were more apt to turn toward an older peer than seek an adult or teacher. She acknowledged that through the process of that normalization, children were more apt to coordinate and cooperate with each other.

After many years of working in Rome, Montessori made her way to the United States. In 1913, Montessori, working alongside Alexander Graham Bell and his wife, founded America's first Montessori Association. The Montessori Educational Association is still the primarily recognized Montessori Authority in America. Montessori did not stay in the United States, but did visit again in 1915 as part of the Panama Pacific International Exhibition. At this exhibition in 1915, she unveiled The Glass House classroom exhibit. She was furthering the idea that observation and not being acknowledged or seen by the children was the best way to see children thrive in their natural habitat.

Montessori kept pushing for change within education systems and awareness across the globe. She was shining a spotlight, not only on all the things that were widely done wrong, but also on all the ways that communities and educators could change education in a positive way for the children.

In 1917, Spain invited Maria Montessori to open a research institute. The government requested that she spend time establishing an institute where children could learn the Montessori method. Montessori obliged and opened the Spanish Research Institute that year. In 1919, Montessori made her way to England. In London, she hosted a series of teacher courses in London where educators could receive training on child psychiatry and the Montessori method. The United Kingdom appointed Montessori as a government inspector of schools in 1922. In 1929, Montessori saw a new level of success as she opened the Association Montessori International, or AMI.

During her travels and between her major successful milestones, Montessori was well known for returning to her home in Italy. Unfortunately, Maria Montessori was driven out of Italy in 1934 for opposing Mussolini. Some also say that she spent the remainder of her life traveling across Europe and occasionally visiting the United States. However, she could never return to Italy.

In 1938, the first Montessori Training Center opened in the Netherlands, and in 1939 India began a series of training courses. Montessori's last major milestone in expanding her education Empire was 1949 when London finally opened its first Montessori Center. Although Montessori was welcomed in the United Kingdom and had served in different positions within the education community, she hadn't been able to get a Montessori Center off the ground. This final achievement, founding the Montessori Center in London, shortly preceded her first nomination for the Nobel Peace Prize.

Following the death of Maria Montessori, there was a lot of scrutiny and changes to the name "Montessori." Mario Montessori, her son (and often collaborator), handled the foundations differently than Maria Montessori. Ultimately, absent copyrights or other protection, almost every country could open Montessori schools, and anyone could use the term "Montessori."

As of 2020, there were over 20,000 Montessori schools internationally, with the United States playing host to 5,000. However, only 1,100 are recognized by the Montessori Educational Association.

Three Components of the Montessori Education Method

There are three vital elements of the Montessori education method. As we mentioned, almost anyone can use the name *Montessori*, but if you notice that any of the three Montessori elements are missing, then it's not true Montessori education. These elements are the adult, often called the directress or teacher, the environment, and the apparatus.

The adult in your situation, most likely the parent, has to prepare themselves before they work directly with the children. The adult needs to understand what passive guidance means. Adults should not be forceful or authoritative, which is a huge challenge for parents. Parents often face scrutiny no matter what they do. If they don't step in during a baby fight or when children have problems, then someone always has something to say. If they do step in, someone also has something to say. There is no "right" way to appease everyone, and with the Montessori Method, teachers and parents choose the less forceful or authoritative approach. So, you'll model the behavior you want them to learn, such as good manners and peaceful interaction. Adults in the Montessori circle are more of a guide or mentor rather than a dictator.

Special note on changing roles: homeschooling or using Montessori at home means that you're more than a parent or caregiver, but think back to past times when this was the norm. Our separation between parenting and teaching is recent, and something you can overcome. You can love, nurture, and create a substantial learning environment. You can also discipline and help your child understand what is and what is not acceptable. It's tough at first, but after the first six months to a year, it gets much easier.

The Montessori environment is a prepared space that encourages exploration and engagement. This environment invites toddlers and young children to touch, make noise, move items, and to live actively within their environment. Ideally, in the Montessori environment, any child can perform any of their daily activities independently or with minimal assistance. For example, they should have access to their clothing, toys, bed, and other areas of their living space. In another chapter, we cover exactly how to build a positive Montessori environment right in your home. It is not a replica of what you would find in a Montessori classroom, but it can help promote independence and exploration with your toddler. And the Montessori environment should, above all else, focus on safety. Through using size-appropriate furniture and removing common dangers, your child can feel safe in the household. You'll also find some relief in not trying to rush in every other moment because something is teetering, or something feels unsafe.

Initially called the Montessori apparatus, this element refers specifically to Montessori approved tools and materials. Because of limited protection on the title Montessori, you might find many toys and furnishings that claim to fall in line with Montessori practices but aren't part of the Montessori apparatus. The Montessori apparatus refers specifically to sensorial materials, namely popular toys such as the Pink Tower, the sorting bears, sound tubes, and some other tools. Maria Montessori refers to these toys as tools and materials rather than playthings. You'll notice that most of these toys are wooden, and most of them are open play or designed for limitless play. They may have an intended purpose, such as The Pink Tower, which was meant for stacking. However, there's nothing wrong with playing with it in many other ways. In different chapters of this book will talk about tools that are specific to that activity or section of development.

Real-Life Stories of the Montessori System and Components

Montessori schools across the world have produced world-renowned artists, businesspeople, musicians, engineers, and leaders in the tech industry. Many of these successful people credit their time spent in Montessori education and emphasize the importance of creativity and exploration. Each of these people has given a fair amount of attention to the time they spent under Montessori style education, and some have directly credited it with the early development of their interests.

Famous Montessori Success Stories

Will Wright created The Sims, a highly successful game franchise through the Maxis and Electronic Arts labels. Wright performed a TEDx Talk that directly addressed how the

Montessori education he had as a young child inspired him to build open-ended games. The Sims was among the first of its kind as a "sandbox" game without an end-goal and instead focuses on life lessons. Wright does acknowledge that architecture and architectural design always interested him, and it lent itself to The Sims design. The TEDx Talk talked about the gaming communities, an overwhelming amount of shooters, and guided-story games. While true, Wright didn't speak out against his fellow developers and engineers. Instead, he simply continued developing The Sims.

Jeff Bezos stands among a small circle of businesspeople who've led a company to such heights of success. However, he's among an even smaller circle of people who've taken a company from three years of extreme debt into the success that Amazon is today. Jeff Bezos, CEO and creator of Amazon not only attended and clearly benefited from Montessori education but is a very public proponent. In 2018, Bezos announced that he would use $2 billion to help aid struggling families and develop an accessible preschool network. By September 2018, he had made good on the first half of his promise by investing $1 billion into opening new Montessori-inspired schools in areas that needed it most.

Other Montessori success stories include both Google founders, Sergei Brin and Larry Page. In fact, there are an extraordinary number of Montessori-educated people in high positions within the tech industry. So much so that news media outlets have taken to calling them the "Montessori Mafia," and it's clear that it has some weight as many are pouring investments into promoting or opening Montessori-inspired preschools across the nation.

These success stories offer only a touch of insight into what someone can accomplish with the right environment and development early in life. Maria Montessori saw children for what they are: opportunity. Each little person is a ball of opportunity if only we can focus on their interests, curiosity, and developing new and exciting ways to engage that child. With your support, not only as a parent but as a humble leader in the Montessori Method, your child can have that nurturing engagement while learning about the world around them.

Chapter 2: Montessori Principles and Activities

Montessori relies on a handful of fundamental principles which lay out the expectation for different activities. These activities tie into different principles that can help the child and the parent or teacher. Through understanding the application of these tenets, teachers and parents can exercise their understanding together. So, what are the principles?

The Montessori Principles are overarching guides, and, as with most other Montessori elements, they offer as much guidance as confusion. Where many people lose track of the core of Montessori is in the principles. As with many guiding texts, these doctrines can have different interpretations, and some people take them to extremes greater than others. It's always best to keep in mind that Montessori herself meant for these to serve at face value – a what-you-see-is-what-you-get mentality is often best when working with this philosophy. There is no need to overcomplicate, overthink, or overact. Imagine these principles exist only in their most simple state.

The activities work to support that idea. The concept that simplest is best resounds throughout Montessori activities and educational approaches. For each principle, we have explained it in the most transparent way, but also provided a correlating activity and an adaptive explanation for application with toddlers. Toddler discipline can set the stage for early childhood development. By starting the Montessori method earlier in life, these principles can be well-honed and in full use by the time they reach kindergarten age.

Principle: "Teacher Ways and Child Ways" or The Respect Principle

One of the eight principles of the Montessori method is there are teacher ways and child ways. Often this boils down to adult interaction and how much interaction is appropriate. Montessori teachers, or *true Montessori teachers*, should have extensive training and years of practice on how to guide and promote independence while still remaining a teacher.

Put simply, there are ways you do things, and there are ways that children or toddlers do things, and they are different. It is not a my-way-or-the-highway situation and it is also not the difference between right and wrong. It is simply this tiny human perceives the world without the decades of knowledge that you've accumulated. They also see the world from a physically different angle. What seems appropriate or reasonable to a toddler or child may seem outlandish and frustrating to an adult because you not only have a deeper understanding of the way the world works but have an easier time accessing the world.

The point of this principle is that adults should allow children to struggle so they can learn. There is a point where adults should step in before frustration takes over. With toddlers, this is frustrating for the adult involved because they may not know when to ask for help or may be so immersed in building independence they refuse help or don't want it.

It is possible to offer too much guidance, and it is possible to be too absent. This principle is a constant work in progress. Even the most skilled Montessori educators have to return to this principle constantly as their guiding light.

If there is one takeaway from this principle, it is to view your interaction and guidance through the lesson of Goldilocks and the Three Bears. When evaluating your interactions with your child, ask is it too much? Is it too little? Or is it just right? Of course, you must change your perception of what you think is *just right* to what is just right for your toddler.

Example

A great example of this is a toddler learning to dress. A lot of toddlers have strong opinions about their clothes and want independence when getting dressed. Some toddlers would rather be naked all the time. They might hate clothes or feel that clothes are confining or know that putting on clothes means leaving the house and they don't want to do that.

Other toddlers love getting dressed. They might love it so much they demand multiple wardrobe changes throughout the day. They might insist on picking out what they wear, and shake their head no at every offer from their closet or dresser until they reach the last item available.

As an example, we will use Emily. Little Emily loves getting dressed. She loves picking out her own dresses and finding different accessories such as tights, headbands, and bows. Emily loves changing her clothes throughout the day, and sometimes throws a fit or a tantrum that results in three or four wardrobe changes. It is frustrating for her parents, and it's frustrating for Emily.

How can you approach this particularly sore subject through the Montessori principle of child ways and adult ways?

First, to align the environment, the parents involved should give Emily access to her clothes and accessories. It can lead to more mess, but it can also promote independence, and she might choose what she wants to wear the first time she gets dressed instead of changing clothes so often.

Second, unlike outfits that involve full pants, dresses are easy to manage even with small hands. When Emily wants to get dressed in the morning, her parents may hand her the dress she wants and ask her to do it herself. Emily will struggle at first and may need guidance with getting her head into the right hole or sliding her arms up, but this is a skill toddlers can learn quickly.

Third, continue consistency with asking that Emily dress herself, and watch as she tries different ways. If true frustration takes over to where Emily would rather not get dressed, then the adult should step in and provide more guidance.

Now, Emily may not get dressed how her parents dress her. She may put her arms in first and then push the dress over her head. She may put her head in first and then flip her arms into place. Emily might step into the dress from the top down and shimmy it up until it's right.

Returning to this key principle, Emily is doing what makes sense and is most accessible for her. She can find her processes as she grows and spends more time dressing. There are child ways, and there are adult ways; neither is inherently incorrect.

Activity

We are just getting dressed as an example, but let's look at stacking activities. Take blocks of different sizes and shapes, and put them in front of your toddler.

Most adults know that to create some sort of stable structure, you would use the biggest blocks at the bottom, the medium blocks in the middle, and the smallest blocks at the top.

We promise that, at least on the first run, your toddler will not follow that recipe for a sturdy structure. They may not even create a structure. They may create a line of blocks and are not inclined to build upward. A toddler might put the smallest blocks on the bottom, and then put the bigger blocks on top. They may even use the smaller blocks and create a single tower that goes straight up.

Use this activity as an observation opportunity. Later, we'll dive deeper into observation and how to do it properly. This activity is also a great way to exercise your patience and deal with frustrations when your child isn't doing something the way you expect them to do or how you know produces a better result. Let your child play with the blocks and know that they are exercising their way of doing things as they go through this activity.

You might offer more guidance, such as suggesting that you build a castle or make a tower of blocks that goes straight up. This guidance can help you see the different ways they approach these projects.

Principle: Order in Environment and Mind

The environment is a huge factor in the Montessori method and education. However, the person who possibly said it best is neither a Montessori advocate nor an age-old teacher. Ruben, a rising star in personal development and exploring happiness, offered the phrase, "Outer order, inner calm."

Outer order inner calm is as true for toddlers as it is for adults. When the environment is consistent, static, predictable, and in order, it takes mental stress off of any situation that happens in that environment. Your toddler's environment should be both calm and orderly. Toddlers enjoy spacious areas where they can move around, but there's also an underwhelming factor. If you have gone into a Montessori classroom, you might have noticed the minimalistic approach to displaying toys and activities.

Fortunately, this principle is one that you will have to return to again and again. In a later chapter, we explain what you should expect and establish for your child in a Montessori-friendly environment. Once these changes are put into place, you simply have to maintain them. You may occasionally have the urge to change things up or move things around, but once the order is established, you have to pick only up and return things to their place.

Now, most parents struggle to keep general living areas tidy, and following the tornado of mess a toddler leaves behind may make neatness seem like the impossible dream. In our example and the activity provided for this principle, we will dive into exactly how this principle applies to you and your toddler. You are not a one-person maid service picking up after every mess your toddler creates.

This principle builds the foundation for a respectful relationship between adult and child. Remember, keep order in the environment and in mind.

Example

You need not look too far to find an example of how a toddler can set an environment into disorder. Many parents struggle with this particular principle because it seems as though it sets them and their children on opposite sides. We promise it is not you versus your child.

Let's look at an example that should seem very familiar to any parent. A toddler's play area is becoming a disaster; it doesn't matter if their play area is primarily in a living room, a nursery, playroom, or the toddler's bedroom. Deshawna loves playing pretend, and she will drag out every stuffed animal and doll to create elaborate parties. These parties might involve dress-up, fake food, real food, tea sets, movie screenings, and even just general mayhem. At the end of the day, there are countless stuffed animals and dolls scattered throughout the room. Plus, all of the toys or day-to-day objects that got dragged out to be part of the pretend play too.

If your response to Deshawna is frustrated outbursts, you wouldn't be the first parent to lose their temper over such a mess. If your response to Deshawna is to pick it up yourself so you didn't have to deal with the argument, you wouldn't be the first parent to choose the passive approach. When parents face a level-10 mess, they may experience frustration, anger, fall into a weepy puddle on the floor, or completely give up and just let the mess exist until they can mentally deal with it.

A mess from playtime is not the only thing that parents have to concern themselves with, and often this disorder in the environment leads us to disorder in mind. It's no wonder that when confronted with this much and disorder in our physical space that we act irrationally.

Activity

Wait, there are activities to help?

Don't get too excited; this is more of a Mary Poppins (minus the magic) approach. There are Montessori tools that engage children in the cleaning process and teach them life skills for cleaning up after themselves.

Mary Poppins is the one that claimed that every job is a game, but the iconic line of, "Well begun is half done," comes directly from Aristotle. You can take both elements and implement them into your daily cleaning. Involve your toddler in cleaning through every step. You are not only introducing them to the idea that we all have to pick up after ourselves, but you're showing them what you do that contributes to a clean environment. Your toddler may not be on board at first. This is one time where Montessori parents do tend to blend authoritative and modeling approaches.

You need not force your child to clean. But you might put your foot down when it comes to breaking out another toy or starting a new mess before the environment is ready. You can tell your child that until the blocks are put away, the room isn't ready to play in. The phrasing you use in cleaning activities is important. When you're cleaning an area and trying to get your toddler involved, or at least having them patiently observe you while you clean, try these phrases:

- "We can play with _____ faster if you helped clean up."
- "We clean so that we have all this space back."
- "After every mess, we have to clean up."
- "I feel so much better when we're done cleaning, but I don't feel good when our room isn't clean."

For some parents, that language can sound a little pandering, but using "we" and "our" instead of me and you is important. The small changes in a language like this can even follow you into adult conversations. Most fights and arguments revolve around you-centric language. Using shared language offers a degree of mutual respect.

You're acknowledging that this is your space, but it is also a space for your toddler. It is where they live and where they should contribute to cleanliness.

Montessori tools that address this principle are really scaled-down versions of adult cleaning tools. Toddler size brooms are relatively easy to find, and you can swap out dish towels for washcloths, or rip a paper towel in half.

When the right tools are available, most adults find they need not clean on their own for long. When you emphasize the benefits of a clean area, toddlers pick up on the behavior you model. When you model cleanliness, especially with a decent attitude, they will likely jump in to help do the job faster.

Remaining Principles

The remaining principles are largely attributed to the first two big concepts we covered but focus on specific elements of learning and development. Once you have the first two big principles in place, the other principles will come much easier and can offer even more benefits for the child and the parent-child relationship.

Principle: Movement and Cognition

Movement and cognition are most recognizable as normalization. In chapter one, we reference normalization as Montessori's term for children behaving in their natural state. The principle is that movement and cognition should happen in tandem and that by presenting activities that engage both movement and cognition, the child learns better.

The most common example of this is independent playtime. When children are permitted to play independently with whatever toy catches their eye, you can watch them engage in different movement behaviors and see they are thinking through the scientific process. Although it may seem like they're only stacking blocks or spreading beads, they're also thinking... *Why does this work this way? What if I do this differently? How does this work?*

A great activity to promote movement and cognition is bead threading. Another great activity for movement and cognition is sorting. Provide your child with a few different items to sort by color or type and watch how they carefully pick them apart and sort them into different groups.

Principle: Choice

Choice is a massive principal in Montessori teaching, and it addresses both respect for the child and sensitive periods. In an earlier example, we noted the choice of getting dressed and wearing what the child wanted. This is an outstanding example of this principle, as children often feel differently about activities or daily routines when they have a choice in the matter.

You can implement choice into almost any part of your day. But, to get started, make an activity choosing between two items. You can use this again and again throughout the day. Start your day by asking if the child wants to wear the red shirt or the blue shirt. Then when it's bath time, ask if they would like the white towel or the brown towel. You can even bring this into eating. Does your child prefer apples or grapes? Maybe they would rather sit in their highchair than at their tiny table. With the activity of presenting toys, start with only two choices. Toddlers are learning a lot, and they're easily overwhelmed with choices. By presenting four or five different shirts or having *anything* in the refrigerator as an option, they may experience choice paralysis.

Principle: Absorbent Mind

The absorbent mind largely relies on children learning through experience, and by learning through experience, they develop agency, independence, and confidence. This largely plays into the first principle. However, it takes a different angle about independence and learning.

Instead of acknowledging the adult way and the child way, this is more about adult restriction. Restrain the urge to say *no* or to speed up a process because something is taking too long. The activity here is more for the adult. Try carrying around a small notebook or even use a tally counter on your phone. Then, mark a tally each time you felt the need to interject into what your child was doing. You can go the extra mile and make notes about why the interjection wasn't necessary, but you'll get the message loud and clear at the end of the day when you have a page full of tally marks.

Chapter 3: Changing Your Perception

Before we can dive directly into implementing Montessori methods and activities, we need to re-evaluate our perception. Teenagers often complain that adults have forgotten what it was like to be a teenager, but toddlers don't even have the communication skills or insight to explain that. We don't know what it was like to live like a toddler; most of us have forgotten. And most of us have little empathy for how children and toddlers view their world and how our perception towards education and learning impact them.

The Montessori method largely dispels the notion of punishment, restriction of freedom, and traditional roles of a caretaker. Many parents wish they could put the idea of punishment aside; Montessori also calls for a drastic decrease in encouragement. It's a challenge, no matter which way you look at it. It is a challenge to change your lens on how you view your child and the expectations you set. However, the payoff can be massive. By not praising, and by avoiding discipline, you're able to watch and appreciate your child's natural curiosity and development. This may be one of the more difficult chapters, and you might need to return to it again and again because changing our perception as parents and adults does not come easily.

Quick Insight Into Brain Development from 1 to 3 Years of Age

Most parents have experienced a long path during pregnancy and infancy and know that, to some degree, what they do affects their child. Childhood development is so malleable, and as parents we know that but, still, we are only human. So, what do toddlers experience between the ages of one and three regarding brain development?

Brain development is possibly at its peak during the toddler years. Toddlers understand and remember shapes, size, color, routine, numbers, songs, animals, and more. They are taking all the sensory exploration from infancy and actually putting it into practice. Positive and negative experiences will directly affect brain development. These experiences will affect them as much as proper nutrition. By the time a child reaches age six, their brain has gained about four pounds in weight and developed between 75 and 90 percent of its complete adult brain weight. Their brains develop about 700 new neuron connections per minute. That is incredible!

However, so much of the toddler's brain is still developing. The prefrontal cortex is not developed enough for anyone at that age to make reasonable or logic-based decisions. Additionally, the limbic system is still running the show. The limbic system is the part of the brain that operates at its most basic state. Hunger, sleep, and more are what come from the limbic system, and because of their irrational processing center, it is easy for the toddler to quickly "lose it," especially over food, sleep, or wanting to do something "their" way.

Toddlers are in stage two of brain development where they're working on reasoning, perception, attachment, emotional understanding, working memory, and life experiences.

Understanding a Child's Perspective on Life

Literally, their entire perspective is different. While you're standing in line at the grocery store, you see the back of the head of the person in front of you. Your child sees that person's pockets, maybe the bottom of the conveyer, and that enticing rack of candy.

Children are usually between three and four feet shorter than standard adults, with smaller hands, smaller steps, and largely, we expect them to just live in our world. As adults, we get irritated when they take too long to tackle a simple task. We walk at a typical pace and aren't inherently astounded these tiny humans can keep up quite often. There's also the frustration that they're so interested in what we're doing that they interject themselves into our activity and simply can't have the same experience. They can't use knives, climb ladders, jump into the deep end without protection, and more. But, as adults, and as people, we're prone to not having easy access to different perspectives. We need to take occasional, purposeful action to dive into the child's perspective. A lot of this you can accomplish by playing with your child and observing them.

They not only see things differently, but they think about things differently. They don't have the knowledge you have, or the height you have, or the tactile abilities for intricate finger movements you have. So, when we can see the world through a child's lens, take that moment and watch them or play.

A Few Specific Things That Impact Your Child Directly

There are things that we heard and experienced as children we are now using in our parental practice. Maria Montessori had a revolutionary impact because of how she broke away from traditional methods of interacting with children of all ages. Here are a few things that often come from the parenting perspective not entirely considerate of the child's perspective. Some of these seem innate, things we do naturally, and feel natural as an adult. Others are something we may have let slip. Either way, here are a few of the most common situations that can affect the child's perception of the world around them, and changing these behaviors could help you understand the child's perception of life.

"Good Girl/Boy/They/Person"

Telling a child they are good is not inherently a bad thing. However, using the phrase sparingly or only when they seem to do what you want, could be causing harm. If you ask them to take a seat to eat their meal and acknowledge that they're a good girl or a good boy, it ties obedience to good behavior. For many parents, that's perfectly acceptable, and most parents strive to have their children listen to them. Having a child listen to you as a parent can be a matter of safety. If your child darts towards the street and you say *stop*, and they stopped, it could have saved their life. However, the question comes up of how obedient do you want your child to be with other adults? Do you want an adult you don't know telling your kid they are a good girl or a good boy and going through behavior that is inappropriate or unacceptable or maybe just not in line with your parenting? Probably not.

There is another problem with the good girl and good boy terms. Going beyond obedience and listening blindly, there's the matter of the unsaid factor of this phrase. If they are good, sometimes it means they are also bad.

If you say "good girl" when your child is listening, then it means that they're not good when they're not listening. However, a child exploring something or having a curiosity that doesn't fit in line with social norms isn't behaving badly. They're doing what their brain is supposed to do at that age. Their brain is expanding and developing rapidly during these three to five years, and exploration and curiosity are the driving elements of that development.

"That's Dangerous" - When It's Really Not

Most parents are probably prone to this one, and they may not even realize how it's affecting their child's perception of the world around them. We often say that something is dangerous when maybe it's really not. Touching a hot plate will deliver a burn, but it's not going to deliver a second-degree burn or a third-degree burn. Just the same as when a child picks up a pair of scissors that can become dangerous, but the overall reaction of jumping in and ripping the scissors out of the child's hand can cause more harm than simply asking for them to put the scissors down. If they don't listen and respond appropriately to request such as putting sharp objects down or handing them to you nicely, then change direction and be a little more assertive.

Often, we respond that something is dangerous when maybe it would just cause very mild harm or discomfort, and it's usually because we just don't want them to do what they are doing. We don't want children to touch the oven door, even though the oven door doesn't get that hot. We don't want them to walk on the edge of the sidewalk because we inherently feel that the next step is to leave the sidewalk. We're scolding them now rather than holding them when they do actually do something dangerous. This comes from good intentions. We see the possible dangers ahead, but our children live in the present moment. Toddlers are not worried about the consequences of moving from the edge of the sidewalk to stepping onto the road because all they're worried about is walking on the edge of the sidewalk.

One of the best Montessori methods that comes with handling possibly dangerous activity or something that could potentially cause discomfort is redirection. Redirection allows the adult in the situation to acknowledge the child's behavior and then pull their attention to something else. You're kind of extorting how much toddlers are immersed at the moment. Let's look at the sidewalk example. You're walking to check the mail when your toddler keeps veering for the very edge of the sidewalk, and you're getting a little nervous. You might have acknowledged how fun it is to walk on the edge but then draw their attention to the flowers growing at the edge of your neighbor's property or how exciting it is to get closer and closer to the mailbox. You might let them hold the mail key or ask if they would like to carry the mail on the way back home.

If these don't sound engaging or if they're too forward-thinking for your toddler at this point in time, you might simply redirect their attention to the elements of nature or their immediate surroundings. You can say, "Wow, look at the bird" or even "Hey, the sidewalk is gray, did you see that?"

Tantrums

Tantrums and toddlers go together like peas and carrots, cheese and burgers, potatoes and gravy. You simply can't separate them. Some children are more prone to tantrums and some are more strong-willed or rebellious. But some children rarely have tantrums or are easy going, so tantrums come quickly and subside just as fast.

Covering tantrums also falls under the element of discipline, which we cover in a later chapter. Acknowledging tantrums so far as the child's perception, however, means looking at things from a different angle. Why is your child throwing a tantrum? Because they didn't get their way? Don't you get frustrated when you don't get to your way? Haven't we all seen various viral videos of adults acting like toddlers because they didn't get what they wanted?

Children don't just throw tantrums because they don't get their way. Many toddler tantrums happen because they are communicating basic needs. In their brains, the prefrontal cortex, the decision center, is still under construction. Your child's behavior and wants is largely controlled by their limbic system. That limbic system manages to control basic human needs. Food, water, shelter, and security are the four primary issues of day-to-day life that the limbic system handles. So, if this is the primary ruler of the toddler's brain, then it is more likely that your toddler is throwing a tantrum because one of these four elements isn't met. They could be hungry, thirsty, want to go inside, want to go outside, or feel insecure at that moment.

There are a few different ways to handle tantrums, and some will be covered in the discipline section, but it's worth mentioning it in the *child perception* chapter. The first is to repeat what the child is doing or saying. Some parents have moved towards using the front-facing camera on their phones to show their children what they look like in tantrum mode. By recreating, mimicking, or outright showing your toddler what they look like in the tantrum, even your toddler can understand this communication is not effective. It can take a while, but repeating what they are saying can help draw attention to the communication breakdown.

For example, Don was quietly playing with his cars, and then his world stopped. Don's mom didn't understand what was going on, but she acknowledged that he began throwing his toys across the room and screaming at the top of his lungs. It was a full-fledged tantrum, and the parent has no idea why it started or how to make it stop after a few minutes of handing cars back to the toddler, offering a sippy cup, and attempting to negotiate. The parent loses her cool, points the finger at the toddler, and says, "That is enough. You need to calm down." Does this sound familiar? It is a pretty standard response for an adult who has to handle multiple toddler tantrums per day that can last between 20 seconds and 45 minutes or longer. At some point, we become less empathetic to their perception, especially in highly emotional situations like a tantrum.

What are the tricks of handling a tantrum? The one we mentioned earlier doesn't come from the Montessori method, but instead from <u>The Happiest Toddler on the Block</u>. By repeating exactly what the child is saying, you'll notice that either the child will begin mimicking you, and a classic Daffy Duck and Bugs Bunny "Yes - no - yes - no (turnaround) no - yes" situation. Or your child will begin to use different words, clearly frustrated that you don't understand or that you're not saying what they believe they are saying.

Now, if repeating what your child is saying doesn't work to deescalate the tantrum - because nothing is a foolproof approach with toddlers - you can try ignoring. Rather than telling the child they need to get it together and calm down, you simply acknowledge that you don't feel good either, so you will give them a moment to feel better, and you'll come back when you feel better.

Your Role as a Parent, Caregiver, and Montessori Teacher

Montessori drastically changes what we consider "normal" parenting practices. There are a million and one different ways to raise children, and most are acceptable. But the Montessori approach takes a more nurturing-approach than a direct tactic. You can still be a parent and not just a teacher. You'll likely find that after some adjustment, you may enjoy the time you spend with your child even more by applying the Montessori perception when working as a parent.

Most parents struggle with the adjustment of declining their level of discipline and taking down their level of praise. Praising is discouraged, and there is solid reasoning behind that approach. The issue is that you want the child to explore their interests, not only the interests you praise them for. And the decrease in discipline isn't necessary to let them free-range raise themselves, but to better understand natural consequences and that natural consequences exist in the world.

As a parent, one of the most challenging elements is to balance our roles. We may be a spouse, caregiver, teacher, mother, father, or parent in some other capacity. Then there is the element of personal neglect, where most parents acknowledge that they simply don't have time to decompress or sit down and watch or read something that interests them. To mildly address this, while also brushing up on the Montessori method, we offer this: as a parent, you are already a teacher.

The idea that you and some other unknown person are both necessary to teach your child is not exactly on point. Now, other adults will have many things to instruct your children, and your child will, without a doubt, learn much from their peers. You will probably need to rely on other adults to cover some topics that you may not know or have expertise in. However, you can always teach your child, and simply through doing and existing, your child is constantly learning from you.

Chapter 4: Observing Your Child

Early in life, we spend hours just watching our babies. However, when they get to toddler age, we start distancing ourselves and become less observant. There are terms such as "follow the child," and "freedom" or "leading" that are often misunderstood in Montessori. So, what do these terms mean, and how can you start observing your child? This chapter will cover everything you need to get over the challenges of understanding your child and how to know when to employ these methods.

Just as with most Montessori terms, the ones involved in observation require a bit of teasing out. We will start with the terms, cover the processes, and then dive directly into the directions of how to observe your child with the Montessori lens.

The Instruction Manual Every Parent Dreams Of

How many parents have you heard say something to the effect of, "Gee, I wish kids came with manuals." Without a doubt, many more parents have thought this and not voiced it. Observation is that sought after instruction manual. By closely observing your child at different points in the day, you'll not only notice what sparked their interest but also what they tend to gravitate toward and what they tend to repel.

Observing is difficult for parents. We're biased and prone to thinking our child is just the most fascinating thing, or we're so utterly overwhelmed with all the other demands of parenting that we can't appreciate those moments that we should be observing. Fortunately, you can plan times for observation or conduct your observation when you have a few moments to sit down and simply watch your kid. We don't mean watching in the sense of babysitting and making sure that they don't get into mischief. You'll soon see exactly what we mean by watching and observing.

Let's Sort Out These Confusing Terms

Following the child—The misconception is this means you just trail along to wherever the kid goes. Following the child actually addresses a larger concept. It means establishing a space developmentally appropriate and offers a variety of interests. Often, you don't need to physically shadow the toddler, but instead visually track how they progressed around the room and what captures their interest or attention the most.

Freedom—The use of the word freedom is possibly the most misunderstood term in all the Montessori practices. The idea that Maria Montessori presented was *freedom with limits*. Those limits are put in place environmentally so that often dangerous or questionable activities simply aren't available. Of course, there's always a limit to what children can or should do.

Example: Tim likes to climb. At the playground, and outside, that is fine. However, during an observation period, Tim's dad saw him climb up onto his small play table. Tim's dad was observing but knew that he had to interject because the play table was certainly not sturdy enough to hold the three-year-old's weight for a long. Tim's dad stepped in and offered that they could take their playtime outside where Tim could climb. Timmy's freedom wasn't compromised; his safety was protected. By moving the playtime outside where Tim could climb, he was continuing to exercise his freedom and to build his motor skills in an appropriate environment. That is freedom with limits.

Leading—There are dos and don'ts with leading with Montessori. Ideally, the child will do as much leading as possible. When the adult leads, much of the independence and experimentation are lost. During observation times leading should be at an minimum, and intervention should only happen when the child's safety is at risk, or they are clearly breaking pre-defined rules. Rules such as "only using nice touching" and similar aren't negotiable just because the child is leading.

Understanding Schemas and Sensitive Moods

These are the moments when your child is immovably interested or invested in what they're doing. Schemas, or sensitive moods, can happen at any point, including when they're not necessarily playing with their toys. A toddler may become incessantly involved with their fingernails, or very invested in the prongs of one of their forks.

Now, these moods come in the ways that a creative muse might. They're not predictable, and they are usually not on any type of schedule. So, you may not always capture a toddler or young child in the moment of a schema or sensitive mood during your observation. That is fine, but do take note that if you see your child in a sensitive mood, it may be the time to start an observation.

What you're looking for to determine if your child is in the midst of a schema is the intense focus. Often toddlers cannot innately focus on one thing for long periods. So, if you see that happening, it is not a common instance, and it's a great opportunity to discover what is engaging your child and question why it's holding their attention so well.

Eight Stages of Observation

If you're not observing, then you don't have a starting point. You don't know where you're affecting the child because you don't know where the starting line is, and that is an critical error for anyone using the Montessori Method.

You'll know where you're starting and how an activity or interaction impacts the child and whether it was positive or negative for that child. These eight stages of observation break down the key points in watching and following children, and it can drastically affect how you engage with them.

Stage One: When giving a lesson, you have the illusion of concentration. You may have a high level of awareness – but it's not actual observation.

Stage Two: Mobile observation. You aren't trying to give a lesson or teach something, but instead are watching on the move. The struggle here is that you don't have context for the activity you might interrupt, and any redirection or interruption you do give is not heeded because the child knows you're on the move. "Why stop what I'm doing when she's not coming back for a while?"

Stage Three: Taking a post. Understanding you have to stop walking and give a few moments for observation. This often results in a ton of frustration because you're "watching" but only taking note of things that bother you, or cultivating internal criticism or correction that builds up into stress.

Stage Four: Sitting and intervening. You know that mobile observation doesn't work, and taking a post resulted in frustration, so now you're telling children to come to you when you see something you don't like.

Stage Five: "Stink-eye" or using a disapproving look to "intervene" instead of physically or verbally intervening.

Stage Six: The "feeling good" stage. Children are coming to you with questions and demands, and you're responding.

Stage Seven: The "almost there" stage. A favorite Disney number, and the last stretch of getting used to observation: you're almost there. In this stage of observation, they can see you, you can see them, and they know you're there to watch, not interact. But you still give in to some questions and acknowledge issues when they arise.

Stage Eight: Observe as an observer. You're not interrupted, either because the child knows not to interrupt or because you're not acknowledging the interruption.

Step One: Sit and Watch

The Montessori method adopts the same techniques of observation that scientists use in field studies. You want to observe your child in their habitat with no interruptions and no interjections. Occasionally, if safety seems to be an issue, then it is time to interject. When we ran through the eight stages of observation, that is the natural progression of someone going from an unskilled or untrained level of observing to a skilled and well-honed observer.

Sitting and watching is difficult, especially for parents. The Montessori method excels in classrooms and learning centers because the adults there don't have the same attachment as you do. They may still love the children or find them fascinating. But, as parents, we feel the need to jump in when we see the child doing something that we believe is wrong. This can be playing with a toy so it wasn't intended by the manufacturer, or something outside of social norms. So, yes, it is challenging to sit and remain motionless, but the first stage of observation calls for that.

While you are sitting and watching, your body may seem emotionless and detached, but your mind should be outstandingly busy. Often, Montessori teachers note that observation is one of the most mentally demanding parts of their day.

Here are a few things that you'll want to remember or think through as you are beginning your observations:

- How often did you want to interrupt your child?
- Would that/those interruption(s) have been necessary?
- How did the child continue after hanging back or hesitating?
- What is the child exploring or trying to accomplish with their task?
- How often did you stop yourself from saying, *hey, don't,* or *no*?

These areas of interest are the biggest point of focus for parents of toddlers and babies. Toddlers are in a state of constant learning, and when we interject or step in and say no, then we're breaking that learning process. By sitting back for a while and watching how your child handles disappointment, frustration, curiosity, and other factors you might have stepped in on, you'll learn that they can do a lot. And they can do a lot that is still within the general social norms.

If you're not sure where to start, then break down your observations into a more structured analysis.

Those who are new to observing and maybe have a problem sitting still for long periods, can take a more analytical approach. Although eventually, you must give it go, you can start by taking notes. Use a small notepad and pen to keep a tally of how often you wanted to interrupt your child. Maybe take a few brief notes about how your child responded in different situations, and what areas of the room kept their interest for longer periods.

Step Two: Repeat Observations in Different Parts of the Home

Most children spend a fair amount of time in their bedroom, nursery, or maybe a shared area such as a living room. However, you may notice that their interests peak in the kitchen or even the bathroom. These are great times to observe as you can explore new interactions that might not be available in their normal play area.

Observation works best when observing the child at observation stage 7 or 8 in various elements. You might schedule observations, or observe when the moment strikes. Trying to ensure that you're not observing your child only in one environment, and only when they're doing one or two activities.

You also want the opportunity to see how well they function in different environments. It's a good way to test some of your elements in the environment. Observing your child in the kitchen can help you know if they can easily access all of their utensils or easily get up to wash their hands. Watching them in the bathroom or a bedroom can help you know what they can and can't access while playing or exploring.

Try to observe in each room of your home and outdoors. Parks or even just the backyard are great areas for observation. You know that for the sake of safety, you're keeping a very close eye on them. But at the same time, you can sit back and watch what elements of nature grab your child's attention. What are they fascinated with outside? Do they move near plant life and animals with ease or hesitancy? Is there a curiosity with sensory play, such as touching dirt or pulling leaves off of flowers?

Let your child loose and watch what they run to, what they explore, and where they spend their curiosity.

Step Three: Critically Reflect on Your Observations to Assess Readiness, Interests, and Needs

A ton of observation work is introspective. Understanding or noticing how often you want to interrupt, or jump can help you drastically change exactly how you interact with the child. It can also change how you perceive your environment. It is a challenge to understand an environment from the viewpoint of a toddler, but observations are the key to gaining the perception.

You may also notice clear cues that your child was hungry, thirsty, or wanted a buddy to play with. Without observation, that would have been easily overlooked. Often parents grow exceptionally frustrated at how children screech, whine or say "*uhn*" for everything. However, these are the flags or cues that parents often note they just don't understand. That ever eluding handbook for handling your baby, toddler, or child could be unlocked during observations.

A final purpose in observation is readiness assessment and interest assessment. Wondering what toys to get next, or if your child is ready to move on in their sensory play? Can they properly hold something steadily? Then it might be time to introduce water play. If they can suddenly pick up small items and aren't inclined to put them in their mouth, they could be ready for sorting activities.

Remember that observation periods should help you understand exactly where to go with the environment's direction, and how to help your child grow. This can help you assess when you feel the need to jump in and start back to see if perhaps the child can handle the situation independently. Observation is a critical point of the Montessori method. Most Montessori teachers acknowledge that if there were anything they could have more time doing, it would be doing observations.

Are you struggling to find time to fit in an observation period? Your alterations don't have to last for 30 minutes or an hour. You can take 10 or 15 minutes to sit and watch quietly. It is best if you can find a time when your child doesn't even see you. Passing by their room when they are playing and stopping in the doorway and just watching them play for 5 or 10 minutes is a great observation session.

Finally, let's end on a note of progress, not perfection. You need not have a perfect observation session. The idea is that you're starting your observations now, and in a few weeks or months, you'll have outstanding and rewarding observation sessions. Start now with what you have, and develop the observation skills so that further down the line, you can watch for 10 or 15 minutes, or even an hour, and walk away with significant information.

Chapter 5: Setting Up Your Montessori Home

Through the first four chapters, you have seen a brief mention of environment. The environment or the prepared environment is a critical point in the Montessori method. There's the idea of an orderly environment, and that the environment itself should provide engagement and cultivate curiosity. But how do you make that happen? Before you can dive headlong into the Montessori method and lifestyle, you need to get your home in order. Your home may be impeccable right now, but it might not be right for the tiny human in your home. Your house can cater to both adults and children, and in doing that, you'll likely create a safer environment too.

There are near-endless ways to create a more Montessori home. A Montessori home should:

1. Incorporate lessons that involve movement and spark interest.

2. Involve children in building life skills.

3. Allow your child to make mistakes and correct the mistakes themselves.

4. Isolate skills and concepts to create a foundation of knowledge

5. Thoughtful design to foster independence.

With these ideas, you can take immediate action. You can walk into your living room and assess the space and probably pick out five or six things you could remove, move, or at least make safer. Because one of the primary driving forces within the Montessori method is an independent exploration, you generally want to reduce the number of times you have to say no or jump in to take something away from the child. This isn't necessarily about putting cabinet locks on and making it impossible for toddlers to turn doorknobs. There is basic safety. Then there is the step of eliminating potential dangers by reducing potential harm.

While having a lock on the toilet seat might make sense if you're worried about your toddler getting into the toilet, the Montessori home looks at ways that parents intervene when they shouldn't have to because there's a reasonable alternative. For example, if you have glass knick-knacks out that you're constantly taking away from your child, they might serve better on a high shelf. Then replace those items with things that the toddler can pick up and touch and turn around and handle.

Assess Your Space

How do you get started? Start by assessing at face value. Sit down in the center of your living room or in your child's playroom or in your bedroom and look at the room from a seed of perspective. Remember that toddlers are typically much smaller than us, and they can see and get into things that never thought as an issue. That is until they pick it up, and we see them with it, and now we have to tell them "*no*" or "*stop*." You know the drill.

Start in each room by sitting and looking through the things that your toddler could and probably will get into. Then take a minute to look at all the things they can't reach. What items up high that could pique their curiosity and possibly Inspire climbing? Think through and identify a few items that your child can pick up and play with or get into without interjection.

Finally, look at the practical elements of the space. Does your toddler have somewhere comfortable to sit or to lounge in your living room? Can they get onto their bed, or do they need help? Can they access drawers that contain their items, such as their clothing or toys?

Room by Room Montessori Style

Let's go through each room and assess what they can or should look like. Many Montessori schools look very similar because some foundational elements make it easy to recreate each room with a Montessori aesthetic.

Kitchen

The kitchen is a big room for Montessori parents and households that adopt the Montessori method. Maria Montessori emphasized that life skills are vital, and we should start life-skill development as early as possible. That means learning to cook, clean up, wash your hands, and organize or put things. This development need not happen exclusively in the kitchen, but the kitchen will be an important room for helping your toddler develop very basic life skills.

To get started, you can bring a stepladder into the kitchen. A step ladder will give your child access to the sink and a better view of the counter. If your child is tall and a simple step stool will do then, that's fine, but a step ladder gives them a little more height.

Then look at the tools and items that your child will use. Toddlers usually have their own set of utensils, plates, bowls, cups, and even snacks. You can put all of your toddler's kitchen items in a drawer on a pantry shelf they can easily access. It is beneficial to do this as most children will identify this accessibility as a better way of communication for being hungry or thirsty. Instead of throwing a tantrum or having trouble communicating their needs, they will often revert to going to the kitchen and getting a plate or getting a cup to acknowledge their fundamental need for food or a drink.

Putting their utensils and kitchen items where they can reach also encourages them to put away their own items. When you're unloading the dishwasher or the drying rack, you can hand them their utensils and plates so they can put them away.

As you introduce cleaning, the kitchen plays a very important role. Most people keep their cleaning products there, and you can do that for your toddler. Having a washcloth, and maybe a spray bottle of water with a lemon rind can make them part of the cleaning process. You can also have a small broom and dustpan available, so that when they drop something, they can quickly get their cleaning items and pick up after themselves. For most toddlers, this is a game, and it's a very fun one because they're mimicking something they've seen you do a thousand times that they've never had the tools to do themselves.

Bedroom/Nursery

Although every other room in the house needs to be accessible and easily usable for adults, a toddler's bedroom or nursery should care more for small hands and small stature. Consider making all toys and supplies available at a toddler's level, always keep their eye level in mind, and give consideration towards their natural inclination to pick up and touch, throw, and generally make a mess. When you place items at their eye level, it also makes it easier to engage them with cleaning activity.

One of the first things to tackle in the toddler's bedroom or nursery, or any room where they spend the most time, is to reduce stimuli. Too many posters, ribbons, decorations, and similar things can pull attention into too many directions at once. Your toddler needs to be engaged and to keep busy, but they shouldn't be overwhelmed.

Now, for art supplies, you can always refer to washable markers, washable crayons, and even Crayola's Color Wonder supplies, which are great as they don't mark on anything other than the special paper. Paint and other messy supplies that you might not want to leave out in the nursery or bedroom can come out during observation periods.

You can also encourage self-care by keeping most things available at their highest that you might otherwise put up higher. Clothes are the primary example here; when a child has access to their wardrobe, then they can pick what they like, and it might be a mess at first, but eventually, they'll lose interest in pulling out their clothes.

Here is a checklist for the bedroom or nursery:

- Keep clothes, toys, and items at toddler level.
- Focus on keeping child-sized furniture with a place for them to sleep, sit, and play.
- Possibly bring in a hand washing station.
- Use low shelves so everything is present and available, rather than drawers.
- Use clear buckets or cubbies to store similar items (blocks, sorting items, etc.).
- Make a system for cleaning or putting away items that even a toddler can understand.

Living Room

Keep some toys or interesting objects out and available at your toddler's reach. Think of items that can always be in the living room and are easy to put away. These items should still offer comfort and engagement. Typically pretend-play items are best for the living room because there are not usually multiple parts, and you can put them all together in one bucket or cubby.

Also, make sure that your little one has space. Consider a small chair for them or an area where they can lounge, especially if they haven't mastered climbing up onto the couch yet. You can also use a specific rug or a play rug to help acknowledge that they also have a space in the living room.

The living room is one of the biggest challenges for reducing interventions. Unlike in the kitchen where you'll constantly watch them, the living room offers enough safety for you to do another task or relax for a moment. Until that moment end because they start pulling down picture frames. Focus on safety and accessibility. Anchor furniture, including TVs, and move dangerous items out of reach or out of the room. Then, look at items you simply don't want them getting into, such as photo albums or meaningful knick-knacks. You might swap out outlets for toddler-safe or "safety" outlets.

The living room should be a place for everyone, and that means your toddler too. Now, they'll grow up quickly, so it's not like moving things to a high-shelf means they'll never see the light of day again. As your children get older, you can relax as they play with items you don't want to be damaged, broken, or lost. Trust is a big element in Montessori, especially as they grow, but at a young age, safety should come first, and you might not want things lost to a tantrum.

Bathroom

The bathroom is another spot with lots of dangers that most people just keep their children away from. It would be easier if your child were only allowed into the bathroom for a bath, using the restroom, and brushing their teeth. However, they also need to wash their hands, and having this as an "off-limits" room in the house is a recipe for potty-training disaster and many tantrums.

To make the bathroom more toddler-friendly:

- Have a step stool or step ladder so they can see and use the sink on their own.
- Use pitchers, plungers, and plastic tubes to promote pouring activities in the tub.
- Encourage bathtub play for sensory development.

What About the Overarching Basics?

There are overarching basics. Keep decor simple and engaging but not distracting. Use rugs on hard flooring, they're great for sensory development, but it's also useful because children will gravitate toward rugs for floor play. Make sure there are accessible items in every room that your child uses for playtime. Encourage them to explore while also maintaining safety with basic child-safety tools.

Wait, don't you need educational materials on every wall? What about the hand washing station in every room? In Montessori classrooms, these make sense, and you can put items up, but you need not make every room in your house look like it belongs in a Montessori center. Your home is also a living environment. In Montessori classrooms and homes, minimalism is a common theme; fewer things, but higher importance on the thoughtfulness of those things and how they are presented.

Chapter 6: Coordination and Sensory Activities

Babies start exercising their coordination of large muscle groups as early as four months old. From that age forward, they develop gross motor skills and fine motor skills, and this is done through coordination activities. A lot of these come up in every day-style child's play. We see kids running in parks, playing soccer, and pulling apart Legos. However, with the Montessori method in mind, there is a way to establish coordination and sensory activities within the toddler's environment to promote positive interaction. You shouldn't have to get up and say, "Hey, let's go outside and kick a ball around." Instead, your child should have access to all the other tools or toys that promote coordination development and sensory building.

Coordination and Sensory in Montessori

What is the Montessori method regarding coordination and sensory play, and how does that help develop muscles and memory? While sensory activities are fun and interesting, they also promote exploration and investigation. You'll notice after some time of working with different sensory activities that your child will begin to turn to the scientific method. They begin by observing, they will estimate what should happen after a certain action, they will experiment, and, after a while, they will draw their own conclusions.

We also know that purposeful sensory development helps build motor skills and nerve connections within the brain. Sensory play also links directly to language development and scientific thinking or problem-solving.

Developing better coordination helps toddlers understand and address problems that involve picking objects up and moving them. Coordination helps children understand how to minimize conflict, understand spatial recognition, and eventually helps them handle daily activities faster. You will sit around waiting forever for your child to put on their own shoes if they haven't properly mastered finger coordination. These coordination activities can do a lot more than what is initially seen. Give them a chance and have fun while you're doing interacting with your child. A lot of these activities do call for interaction by the parent or humble teacher.

Think Beyond the Go-To Activities

We have a ton of fun and engaging activities you can do with a toddler as young as 18-months-old. It might seem that some of these are very advanced, and you can acknowledge that through observations. Even if some of these activities seem beyond your child's immediate development stage, give them a shot and see if they're willing to participate and engage.

Our first activity turns a lot of heads for parents. Catching and throwing it seems like something a five or six-year-old should do. However, many two-year-old's can catch and throw well. Let's get into these activities.

Catch and Throw

Underhand, overhand, from the side, rolling across the floor, you can catch and throw in almost any way possible. It is fun, builds coordination, and there are a lot of endless opportunities to be silly. However, there are a few ways to really amp up this activity.

Consider having a variety of ball sizes as the different sizes will exercise different portions of muscles in your child's hands. If your child doesn't have the catch-and-throw idea down, start with a beach ball. They are light and easy to pick up with two hands. They're also super easy to throw overhead. Then your child gets the big reward of the ball going far because of its weight and can execute a 'proper' throw.

If you don't want to encourage throwing indoors, you might use soft-hit or squishy balls. Otherwise, keep the balls outside for catching and throwing.

Walk with a Lemon

Walking with an egg balanced on a spoon is a favorite of holiday and office parties. However, your slightly less coordinated little person at home can reconstruct this game. Give them a head start on the office parties. To play this game, set a starting point and a finish line. One great way to set these points is to use masking tape, Washi tape, or just simply place start and finish line items on the floor.

The "walk with a lemon" game can work in two ways. First, the toddler can simply hold the spoon while balancing a lemon and walking from the start to the finish point. Second, the toddler can hold the spoon in their mouth. There are a few things to remember if you challenge your toddler to walk with the lemon balancing on a spoon held in their mouth. First, try to avoid using metal spoons for their teeth. Second, use the smallest lemon you can find or fall back to limes because they are much lighter.

The best part of using a lemon rather than an egg is the peace of mind regarding cleaning up. There is nothing about this activity you should have to clean up. Your toddler should be able to return the lemon to its place, put the spoon back, or toss the spoon out if it was plastic, and pick up the start and finish line areas.

Container Bowling

How many Tupperware containers do you have in your cupboard? Tupperware, stacking containers, and even plastic cups all make great pins for bowling. All you need for this activity are a couple of somewhat stackable items and a ball that is heavy or large enough to knock the items over or out of the way.

You may notice that toddlers set up bowling differently than we know the game. Many toddlers will set up their bowling space how we might see the traditional carnival game of knocking over pins or bottles. This setup is acceptable and offers a bigger reward for tipping over items with a successful bowl.

Typically, expect your child to get wildly creative with their bowling setups. It's a great reason why this activity is so great for coordination. They're not just knocking over pins, but also taking the time to place them strategically or stack them upwards.

If you're looking to put together this game with just items from around the house, consider using disposable cups, either Styrofoam or plastic. Your child will have fun stacking the cups up or placing them in a bowling setup, and then they can do almost any size ball, and the cups will tip over.

Stack Containers

The Pink Tower is a well-known Montessori tool. However, you need not buy specific tools to get started with this activity. If you're trying to gauge how interested your toddler is in stacking and similar coordination activities, use items from around the house. Not only will this help build your child's coordination, but it promotes creativity.

How many cups can they stack upward? How many Tupperware containers will nest inside each other? Can they stack books? Is it possible that their animal figurines will stack up too? Stacking containers or nearly any kitchen or bathroom storage device can help toddlers grasp the concept of coordination and facial recognition. They must explore and decide for themselves whether an item will stay stacked on top of the other item or not.

A final note on stacking containers. If you're worried about the toddler stacking things too high, or using items that may be heavy, then you're sitting right there observing. You don't want to interject before it's necessary. This activity is such a great opportunity to watch your child go through the scientific process and use household items to cultivate creative coordination play.

Dry Pouring

Dry pouring is an absolute favorite among Montessori parents and teachers. It is as simple as gathering beans, rice, pasta, sand, moon sand, or even dirt from outside. Because this activity has so many variations, we will include a few tips and tricks to help make it a little more fun too.

So, what is dry pouring? Dry pouring is an exercise or activity that allows the toddler access to a dry material they can scoop and then pour from one container into another. Some parents use sheet pans, pots, storage containers, or buckets. If you have a few buckets from summer, the pails intended for beach use, those are excellent for this activity.

How to Color Beans, Pasta, or Rice for Dry Pouring

- Divide the desired beans, pasta, or rice between three to seven sandwich bags.
- Drop a few drops of food coloring into each bag (you can go from primary colors to the full rainbow). A few drops go a long way!
- Wait for 24-hours for the beans, pasta, or rice to dry.

- Place the beans or rice onto a sheet pan or in bowls.

Moon sand is also excellent for this activity because the child can pour and move the sand in clumps or in its sandy form.

How to Make Moon Sand

1. Place 8 cups of flour into a large bowl or container.

2. Create a crater in the middle of the flour.

3. Pour 1 cup of baby oil into the crater.

4. Mix the oil and flour in a churning and kneading motion

In its final form, the moon sand will still look suspiciously like flour. However, as soon as your little one gets their hands on it, the sand will clump up. Great for pouring and watching something change from an almost rock shape into sand again.

When you're looking for pouring tools, you can go to the tried-and-true measuring cups. However, you can also use sand shovels, bath rinses, spoons, ladles, containers, and cups.

The element of coordination here is to get a generally large amount of the item from one container into another container. This activity is great for outdoor play. Set a plastic planter of dirt in front of your child and watch as they methodically scoop it with a tool and pour it onto the ground. Easy to clean, and most young children will have a prolonged interest in this activity.

Sorting Items

Montessori teachers know and love sorting activities. These activities are straightforward and definitely something you can do at home with little effort. You can use the same beans or rice you had for pouring, for sorting. Making big batches of colored beans, rice, or pasta is an excellent way to switch from one activity to another. Dye your beans, rice, or different pasta colors.

Place the items on a sheet pan or mixed in a bowl. If you're mixing items together in a bowl, you might use beans and pasta rather than rice. Then have your toddler sort these items by color.

Give them the appropriate goals for the number of colors that they're sorting. Allow them to develop their fine motor skills and coordination to pick up these small items and drop them into a bowl. These activities are a great opportunity to build pincer grip strength. You'll notice that your toddler naturally tries to pick up these smaller items between their thumb and forefinger.

One element of sorting activities that stands out from some of these other coordination activities is the focus. Toddlers find bowling and musical instruments engaging. However, sorting items calls for more focus. They have to not only engage tactically but also think strategically about where to place the item and if it's in the correct bowl.

One of the more famous Montessori tools or toys is the Sorting Bears. You can now find sorting bears not only in bear shape but as dinosaurs, chickens, trains, and more. This toy often comes away with around 50 differently colored small-shaped items. Then there are seven cups, each a different color of the rainbow. Usually, with tongs or their fingers, that child will pick up each little bear or dinosaur and place it in the cup that matches its color. You need not invest in this toy right away, or even. If you would rather use household items, that is fine, and some Montessori teachers promote the use of alternative items. If you're stretching your creativity to put together these activities, the child will see that resourcefulness and mimic it.

String Beads or Pasta

A little yarn, large beads, or large size tube-shaped pasta can keep your little one entertained for quite a while. However, this activity can go wrong quickly. When stringing beads or pasta, you need to think about the environment and the tools available. Two-year-old's are typically far past putting things in their mouth. However, even children as old as four or five can do this thinking it is funny, and they're oblivious of the choking hazard.

Yarn is typically better than fine string or even embroidery thread because it's easier for small hands to handle. When looking for beads, you want something larger than Perler Beads. Many parents using Montessori as a model will use large rigatoni or penne pasta. Using pasta can also help children learn to control their pincer grip or their palm grip in that if they drip too hard, they will crush the pasta. Only use pasta in its dry form.

When setting up this activity, you'll want to put restrictions in place. For example, take the yarn down to the table, floor, or play area. You might also create a small enough piece of yarn that the toddler can't wrap it around anything they shouldn't.

Let's make a Deal

Is it possible that your child can learn coordination and develop their decision making? Absolutely! The 'let's make a deal game' is pretty fun, and you can use this game as early as six-months-old. Although six months is a little young regarding toddler discipline, this can help set the stage for decision-making and compromise.

There are a few elements of daily life to consider when putting together this activity. First, this activity requires the participation of the humble teacher or a Montessori parent. This activity does not count as observation, although you'll probably walk away with some good insight into your child's decision-making abilities and personal preferences. Second, you can tailor this game toward things you know your child likes or present new items. Finally, you want to keep a distraction-free environment and try to play this game somewhere there aren't other items your child may want.

So, how does this work?

- Step one, sit your child or toddler down and hand them two items.
- Step two, hold up a new item in front of your child and request they exchange something they're already holding for the new item.

- Step three, repeat the process with new items until your child loses interest.

Now the instructions are straightforward, but they rarely account for some serious deviations happen. As a toddler, your child may cleverly refuse to give up any items and instead take multiple items into their arms or set them in their lap. Mostly, this is acceptable. Ideally, you want them to exchange one item they already had for a new item. However, your child will eventually run out of space and have to start giving-up items to take new items.

Or you could take a different approach and acknowledge that everything is an even exchange. The child cannot have the new until they decide which one they will give up. Whatever approach you choose is up to you; just remember that consistency and fairness are vital to children.

The other issue that comes up during this game is the child not wanting to give up any item and has no interest in the offered item. When the child shows no interest in the offered item, it is okay just to set that item to the side. When you send items to the side, it is an indicator that your child just has zero interest in that thing. Now, because of changing interest, the Montessori parents will use this activity to gauge interest. They may use only kitchen items during one game, and then on a different day, use items that the child often uses. You may do this activity outside and offer different plants or different outdoor toys.

Everyday Instruments

Most adults have seen or heard of very young children or toddlers banging on pots and pans. That is essentially what you're recreating with this activity. Pots, pans, Tupperware, rubber bands, paper towel tubes, and many other household items produce music or at least sound.

When setting up this activity, you might wrap a few thick rubber bands around an open-container or bowl. You might provide a set of wooden spoons and pans that your child can run with or paper towel tubes of different lengths they can blow through.

You can also turn to standard instruments. Recorders, drums, sound tubes, maracas, and tambourines are excellent toddler instruments. Almost every instrument requires proper holding or engagement of the hands and one way or another. Drums evidently call upon coordination, but the sound tubes are an excellent Montessori tool because of how they create different sounds depending on where they are struck.

For these activities, if you are trying to lead a lesson, ask the child to produce different sounds using one instrument. For example, you might shake out one beat with a maraca and ask them to make a different rhythm.

Water Painting

Water painting is an absolute favorite, especially for parents that don't want the mess of painting. You need a stack colored paper only, or butcher's paper, and water. Children can water paint with their fingers, paint brushes, foam brushes, or pom-poms. Pom-poms are a fun variation; they clearly produce different size droplets of water and develop the pincer grip in toddlers.

What's water painting, you might ask? They paint over something you've already put onto the paper. It is a great way to promote tracing and advanced coordination or encourage the development of their alphabet. You can make simple lines, wavy lines, letters, numbers, and much more.

Button Tracing

Similar to water painting, button tracing is a low-mess activity that focuses on coordination development. With button tracing, you'll want to have a variety of button sizes, but nothing so small they could be a choking hazard. Then you must sit down before you start the activity to make a few basic shapes.

To get started with button tracing, take construction paper or printer paper, and create a few designs. Start with only four or five pages. On each page, you can put more than one design, but it's better to keep their focus on one thing when they're new to this activity.

On a single page, you might create a dotted line version of a letter, number, or image. You can create the general outline of a smiley-face or a tree, and then I have a toddler use buttons to cover up the dotted lines and complete the image. Button tracing develops pincer grip, spatial recognition, and sliding.

Chapter 7: Helping Around the House

When your house is set up as a Montessori environment, then you may find it easier to get help around the house. Toddlers naturally want to be helpful, and they want to be around the adults in their life. Although a lot of the Montessori method revolves around children learning from similarly aged peers, there's much they can only learn from you. Cleaning up around the house is a basic life skill, and it's one that every adult needs.

As a bonus for parents, getting a little extra help around the house, but the chores should be micro-chores. You wouldn't ask your toddler to tackle the dishes by themselves. You're also not expecting them to dedicate more than one or two minutes to any particular activity. Sure, some of these will take you a while to complete, but by offering to let them help, they can come and go in the activity as their interest spikes and wanes.

Toddlers can hardly ever accomplish these things with perfection, especially on the first try. But implementing these can drastically reduce your stress in the long-term. Not only because you're getting help with household tasks, but because you know that your child can confidently handle these tasks and they are learning life skills.

What Can Your Child Actually Do?

So, what can your toddler do around the house? The bigger question is actually what they can't do. Your toddler can help you unload the dishwasher, put their plate into the dishwasher, help with laundry, help care for household plants, clean up their toys, pick up small messes, wipe up spills, and even meal prep. A lot of the restrictions we put on small children are simply because we know we can do these tasks faster and with greater effectiveness. However, when we involve these children early, they can quickly improve their skills in these tasks and provide greater help at younger ages. These are life skills that they will have to learn eventually, so why not start early?

Dishes

There are always some restrictions. As Maria Montessori preached, freedom with restrictions is the ideal situation for toddlers and young children. The dishwasher is a great example. If your toddler is helping to unload the dish drying rack or the dishwasher, then you clearly wouldn't be handing them knives to put away. You may also avoid handing over heavy casserole dishes. But they can have a grand time stacking together Tupperware and putting away spoons. When instructing how to help unload the dishwasher, you can teach a toddler how to carry things with two hands and how to ask for help when there's something they can't reach.

Laundry

With handling laundry, there' are a lot of opportunities. Not only can they help put away folded laundry, but they can help sort clothes into piles. They can help by sorting towels, bedding, light-colored clothing and whites, and dark colors. They can also help her clean laundry out of the dryer. If you have a front-loading dryer, this is much easier, but you can still hand them clean items from a top-loading dryer and ask them to put them in the laundry basket.

Cleaning Up Their Toys

Many parents don't ask their children to pick up their own toys until they're four or five years old. Your toddler can learn to clean up their toys as early as one-year-old. The way they will learn is by watching you. You are modeling behavior and constantly asking for support or help. We covered that toddlers love to help, and they also don't like having their things touched.

When you pick up their toys, you can instigate them to help you. Always start by asking for help and acknowledging that it's their mess or their toys.

If your child has reached the age where they like things a particular way, you can make it a game. You can pick up an item and say it loudly that you will put it somewhere it doesn't belong. Then, start walking toward the wrong area where you intend to put down this toy and watch as your toddler springs into action to correct you. You can also play the fool and act as though you don't know where anything goes. You can pick up an item and ask, "oh, does this go in the garage?" or "I think this goes in your sister's room." Toddlers love to correct adults when they know that things work in a specific way. Giving them that opportunity helps build skills for knowledge sharing, and it means you can sit in one spot on the floor, and they'll do most of the actual cleaning.

Small Messes and Spills

Small spills and messes happen every day. If your child is new to using an open container rather than a sippy cup or bottle, they may even happen multiple times per hour. Together you can get past crying over spilled milk when you know that you have help cleaning it up. Arm your toddler with a small stack of washcloths in the kitchen, bathroom, and wherever they play the most.

That way, when a spill happens, they can grab a washcloth, because they know where they are, and immediately soak up the liquid.

With messes, you may have to give a little more guidance. Messes such as crumbles from food might require a vacuum or a broom and dustpan. You can get a child-sized broom and dustpan so the toddler can sweep on their own. They may not always do a good job; they probably will usually do a very good job, but it doesn't make the mess worse. You allow them to try to clean up the mess, and the reward of helping.

Meal Prep and Cooking

Do you remember how old you were when you started cooking? Most of us don't start actively cooking until we move out on our own. However, you can involve your toddler in the cooking process at a young age. Toddlers are excellent at peeling oranges, washing vegetables, and pouring in the pre-measured elements of a meal.

Evidently, there are a wide variety of dangers in the kitchen. From boiling water to knives, it seems as though even the simplest snacks can present immediate peril. Most of this is our own concern because there is a wide variety of activities you can do as long as they have your supervision. If you need to mix or stir something, ask your toddler. They can at least try.

The safest activities in the kitchen for toddlers involve washing vegetables and fruit, peeling fruit with their hands, not with a peeler, and stirring mixtures together. When stirring, they can use a spoon, whisk, or fork, and they often do well. If it seems as though asking your toddler for help in the kitchen means the task taking forever, remember that their short attention spans will quickly have them out of the kitchen. Most toddlers are very happy to find somewhere quiet to play while you continue cooking after only a few minutes of offering their help. There is a type of security that comes with knowing they can return to your side if they want to, but most of the time, they'd rather play independently.

How are "Chores" a Part of Your Child's Montessori Experience?

Chores aren't necessarily the choice word used among the Montessori Community, but let's be honest; it is what it is. Even as adults, we know that doing the dishes and folding laundry are chores. However, we can reframe this unpleasant task for children. Not only can micro chores with your children be fun, but they help to build a respectful relationship. You know that you don't like doing these things, but your child doesn't know these are unpleasant things yet. If more adults worked with teaching these household duties are not chores but instead part of a group contribution to maintaining a proper household, we might have happier adults.

So how do we do this, and how are these household duties part of the Montessori experience? It always starts with tools and invitations. Your toddler cannot hold a full-size broom and use it effectively. To invite your child to help sweep, then get them a tool that's their size. Don't rush out and buy a bunch of household cleaning utensils that are child size. Much of the cleaning can be done purchasing nothing because you can use paper towels, washcloths, spray bottles, and sponges for the majority of your household cleaning.

So, once you have the tools, or have found that item that your toddler can easily handle, you can move into the invitation. The invitation is your extension to your toddler that you will do an activity, and they are welcome to do it with you. This is as easy as asking for help. You might say, "I'm going to get the laundry; can you help me fold?" With the right framing, you can present this as something you'll do together rather than something you will do, and they can leave you alone or be in your way.

Now we mentioned earlier that help us love helping, but toddlers are also destructive even if it's unintentional. How many parents have folded and stacked laundry only to turn around and find their two-year-old throwing folded items up into the air? Even if not every parent has experienced this, I'm willing to bet there are a fair few who know the situation. Pay close attention to the language you use as you follow up on that invitation. Instead of saying get out of the way, you might say excuse me. If they miss a spot, instead of saying, "Oh, you missed blah blah," it might sound better than, "Can I try now?"

The Montessori experience always comes back to freedom with restrictions. The fact is: *the house will not maintain itself.* Another fact is that no single adult should be exclusively responsible for cleaning up after multiple people. Your toddler lives in the house and must eventually learn to help maintain the house. This need not be unpleasant, and don't call them chores, and it need not be a grudging obligation for anyone in the house. When coming back to freedom with restrictions, your toddler has the freedom to help you and to contribute to the house, and in doing that, they'll be a bigger part of the household. The Restriction is that when the environment is not clean or orderly, everyone in the house feels it. Someone has to clean, and if your toddler is choosing not to participate or not to engage in the invitation, then they will find out when they attempt to engage you, and you're doing these activities. At that point, you're busy.

Show, Show, Show, Then Observe, and Always Involve

"Tell me, and I forget, teach me, and I may remember, involve me, and I may learn." This is a well-known quote from Benjamin Franklin. Although he was born long before Maria Montessori introduced the concept of involvement and engagement to children, he had the right idea. You can show and tell your toddler. However,

it's only through involving your child that they'll effectively learn the life skills necessary to maintain a house of their own someday.

As a toddler, you're not expecting them to keep the cogs of the household turning. You're simply expecting them to get involved and to help in a very small capacity. You are not assigning chores to your toddler. You're also not giving them a job to do on a regular basis. Through using Maria Montessori teaching, we know that modeling the behavior we want from our children is the best way to produce desirable results. We know that even when they don't take up our invitation to help in cleaning up if we do it, then they'll see it is part of a daily routine.

Show your toddler how you do each activity, and maybe even narrate the process. Then when they do want to help, take a moment to observe their actions. It's always a benefit to watch how toddlers and children have picked up on so much by just watching us work. But it is not enough to show your toddler and then to observe when they're in action. You need to continue that open line of communication and involvement.

Some parents schedule time for cleaning and acknowledge to their toddler or child that they're welcome to help. Other parents use little moments of time to pick up and again invite their toddlers to help. Either method works. You can be firm or flexible. The important thing here isn't how you do it. It's about involving them in the process and keeping that involvement consistent. Practical life is a driving force among Montessori parents and educators. These are also parts of everyday life, from picking up clothes off the ground to returning objects to their home. They must develop life skills and helping out around the house is a great way to start introducing these elements of practical life.

Chapter 8: Music, Movement, and Montessori

One famous Maria Montessori quote addresses the topic of music directly. It states, "There should be music in the child's environment, just as there does exist in the child's environment spoken speech. In the social environment, the child should be considered, and music should be provided." Maria Montessori states a direct correlation between music, movement, and development. Music is, in itself, a language. However, unlike English, Italian, Spanish, French, or any of the other languages we speak, music brings movement with it. Music ties communication with our physical bodies and these activities explore music and movement so it fits into the Montessori model.

Some of these activities and methods of interaction pull directly from age-old Montessori teaching. Others rely on newer information and tactics and introducing music to toddlers. Either way, music is a great way to have fun.

What Children Learn from Music and Movement

Music improves literacy, numerical sense, sensory development, enhances moods, and physical coordination. Music is also a critical way to build a toddler's vocabulary. Basically, if you're looking to bring the Montessori discipline into your home, music should play a big role in that plan. Music can be a way to redirect children toward positive interactions, or used as a mood lifter, it can make meltdowns easier to handle.

We've known that music has these abilities even at a young age since the time of Plato. Plato said this on children and music:

> *"I would teach children music, physics, and philosophy; but most importantly, music, for the patterns in music and all the arts are the keys to learning."* - Plato

Music provides a delicate balance between mathematics and the physical realm. It accomplishes that balance while fostering creativity and sensory exploration. The experimentation and creation processes of engaging in musical activity are beyond value. It accelerates brain development and sensory development.

Because of children naturally mimicking our moves and behaviors, we can all teach without providing "instruction. Through doing this, our children will watch and model our motions and habits. When building up their interest in music, you only have to start by presenting the tools, resources, and of course, source material.

One important element to address is that don't push kids into sheet music. Although many regarded Mozart as a prodigy, it is more likely that his father, a trained musician, and composer, pushed formal training on him. Don't worry about formal training just yet. Always remember that Montessori teaching and models focus on the child finding what interests them and exploring that interest freely and creatively.

When Did Music Become Part of the Montessori Model?

Auditory sensory development was one of the first major changes that Maria Montessori made after observing children. Children in traditional schools were subjected to different visual stimuli, but the auditory stimulus was significantly lacking. Musical activities were promoted through the years, such as nursery rhymes, bells, easy to handle instruments, and dance. Interpreting music and movement not only addresses the need for auditory sensory development but for developing coordination and gross and fine motor skills.

As with all things of the Montessori model, through the refining and introducing auditory stimulus, Maria Montessori ensured that music and movement created a cooperative learning environment. All the activities mentioned here help create a cooperative and well-organized environment while also promoting independent work and instruction.

Maria Montessori recognized that having music around, with or without words, can help children identify sound patterns and learn because of repetition. Music also helps children learn anticipation and to predict what will come next because of patterns in that repetition. Children that have frequent exposure to music master literacy and numeracy at much younger ages. When linking music with movement and dance, they can increase their skill level and abilities with strength, balance, and muscle development.

Early into developing the Montessori method, it was evident that children's natural love of music and making sound was an integral part of the learning experience.

How to Bring Music Into Your Home

Your home may already have a wealth of music involved. We all saw how quickly songs such as a baby shark took off, and it's evident that parents are still very involved in introducing nursery rhymes and sing songs to their children. However, it is a struggle to bring more music into the home and reduce time with the TV or a screen. Even with smash hits such as Baby Shark and nursery rhymes reimagined through animation with companies such as Super Simple Songs, the child is still in front of a screen.

One element of sensory development that Maria Montessori returned to repeatedly was that such development should attempt to focus on one sense at a time. If at all possible, reduce the time you promote music along with visual stimulus. Even just having music playing in the background can drastically change the mood and feeling of the environment.

Not every music activity has to eliminate screens, and not every music activity requires dance. But relying on activities that do involve movement (or an additional stimulus) can promote engagement with the child. Toddlers are not only naturally curious, but they're natural music makers.

We'll dive into specific activities, but for now, here are a few extremely easy ways to bring music into your home:

- Stream music or the radio whenever possible
- Leave out instruments frequently for interaction.
- Sing what you're doing (It's more common and less weird than you might think!) Really, just narrate what you do in a sing-song voice and listen to your toddler do the same.

When looking for ideas on streaming, you can always tune into a local classical channel or even your favorite radio station. If you use a streaming service, you might search for "happy songs," "toddler songs," or even "happy music." The music should serve as a stimulus, but also as a mood booster. Who doesn't want a happy toddler? Part of tapping into that happy toddler essence is preventive measures, and music could be the key to getting your toddler into a good mood early in the day.

Tools

You want a range of instruments, some that you may need to handle, and others that little hands can easily grasp and interact with daily. And you'll want, for a variety of reasons, a wide range of sounds. There are times when you might turn to softer instruments, but when the kids want to make big sounds. You should have both options available.

For many reasons, most parents do not want the Montessori bells in their homes. There is no blame or shame in not bringing the bells home. Some parents have created DIY Montessori bells and intentionally placed them outside. The Montessori bells are loud and not always pleasant. However, they provide a massive amount of opportunity for exploration within a scale. If you can bring the bells into your home, give them a chance.

Reference this list for possible music and movement tools to bring into your home:

- Xylophones or pentatonic metallophone
- Bongos or conga drums
- Shakers
- Castanets
- Jingle sticks
- Tambourine
- Ukulele
- Sound cylinders
- Tone blocks
- Rain sticks and thunder sticks

Get Toddlers Moving and Grooving with These Montessori Music and Dance Activities

Getting your toddler interested starts with the presentation. If you can, dedicate a shelf to musical items. That shelf should be at your child's level and then place each instrument in a basket or cubby. However, you might also put them all together in one box, or bring them out when you can have more noise in the house.

Once you decide how you'll display or provide the instruments, you can move onto some activities. Some of these are very simple, and others do provide instruction.

Singing Time

You can sing together or take turns. Singing time is a great opportunity to explore turn-taking. But it's also a great way to prompt memory. Start by humming the beginning to a familiar tune and then ask the child to sing the song. You can also use sing-along tracks where the music plays but not the lyrics. It's very much like karaoke.

You can initiate it with a familiar song and then move into singing songs that are new where they can grow their vocabulary and repertoire.

Coordinated Dance

You can accomplish coordinated dance time in a few ways. First, you can put on a YouTube video of a coordinated toddler dance or nursery song such as Baby Shark. Second, you can lead your toddler through dances you might already know, such as I'm a Little Tea Pot.

Coordinated dance should be the introduction to dancing. You might hand the reins over to your toddler once they seem to have it down.

Free Dance

Mats or rugs are excellent for free dance sessions. Set out a yoga mat or dedicate a rug to dancing. Turn on the radio and let them shake, bounce, and disco it out. The best way to conduct dancing activities is to model. The Montessori method relies heavily on the parent or teacher modeling the activity or the behavior. If you're looking for fun ways to connect with your toddler while still using the Montessori method, dancing is a great opportunity.

Walk the Line

You don't need Johnny Cash to walk the line, but walking the line is a fun activity specifically for classical music. Use tape (electrical tape is great for this) and put down one line on the ground. Your line can be straight, a circle, an ampersand, or even a treble clef if you want to get fancy.

Then play classical music and have them move along the line in response to the music. They can move to the beat, to the melody, or just in response to their emotions.

Songs that Engage Movement

Have you heard, "One Little Finger" or "Head Shoulders Knees and Toes?" If so, then you already know a few songs that engage movement. You can get your vibrant and unaware toddler to sing at the top of their lungs while also learning parts of the body and how to follow directions.

One of the major misconceptions in the Montessori Method is there should be no direction given. Even Montessori teachers seem to struggle with this concept as they offer advice such as, "I don't find myself giving instructions often," or "We let the children decide." The toddler can still decide if they want to participate or not, but it's okay to say, "*Watch mom/dad*" and then turn on the song or sing it and do the dance. They can participate or not.

These songs promote engagement, movement, interaction, and body awareness. They're also a ton of fun to do with your child. Music that engages movement isn't really the time for observations.

Try these songs:

- Itsy Bitsy Spider
- Baby Shark
- Stand Up, Sit Down
- This Little Finger
- Party Freeze Dance
- Wiggle It Dance
- The Airplane Song
- Five Little Monkeys

Look up the dance moves, but if you have access to the songs, you can always make up your own dances.

Musicians from Montessori Teaching

Musicians are well known for emerging from Montessori teaching. Unlike the prodigies of old, such as Mozart, these people weren't drilled with fundamental practices. Instead, it's about letting them explore, try new sounds, and learn the physical restrictions regarding music themselves.

Each musician received worldly accolades. Now, there's no guarantee that your child will become an international sensation in any genre. However, the time you spend with your child, allowing your toddler to explore music, can develop a lifelong passion. Music can drastically affect your child if you let it, and these famous people show just that.

Taylor Swift

The first of the Grammy award-winners on our list, Taylor Swift, is a household name. She was announced as country music's youngest-ever Entertainer of the Year and she attended the Alvernia Montessori School, in Berks County, PA. She's widely applauded Montessori teachings for young children and even donated directly to the Montessori school she attended.

Yo-Yo Ma

With 15 Grammy's, a National Medal of the Arts, and recognized as a child prodigy cellist, Yo-Yo Ma stands apart from many musicians. The reason for this? The ability to think outside of traditional definitions and restrictions in music by pursuing his own interest. As a United Nations Peace Ambassador, it's clear that the desire to continue growing and improving his versatility was nurtured early.

Joshua Bell

Award-winning violinist Joshua Bell was also involved in a cultural experiment, which became a Pulitzer prize-winning story. Internationally renowned, Bell began experimenting with music at three, and by four, was playing the violin. He started his education in the Montessori Method. Like many, at some point, he excelled and was placed into standard schooling. Bell's first record came out in 1988, and he is still creating music.

Beyonce Knowles

Beyonce started in Houston, Texas. During her career, she's won 22 Grammy's, appeared in Time Magazine's 100 most influential people in the world, and sold over 100 million records. Her love of music began early. At St. Mary's Montessori School in Houston, Knowles attended classes at a very young age. When she was seven, she won a talent show. She continued at St. Mary's Montessori until third grade and still credits the school for empowering her and fostering her lifelong love of music and learning.

Chapter 9: Learning New Skills the Montessori Way

Learning new skills, including the development of language, speech, reading, numerical sense, writing, and much more, is all possible through Montessori methods. These methods are helpful ways to not only make learning fun but to sneak it in through everyday activities. You won't have to sit your toddler down and say, "Well, today we're learning to write." Instead, the new skill will emerge rather naturally.

The ability to learn new skills and engage in new activities with confidence is one cornerstone of Montessori learning techniques. This factor is also what drives people toward the Montessori model. When you have toilet-trained, two-year-old's and three-year-old's that can write and spell their name, it's pretty impressive. Now, remember that Montessori doesn't advocate for comparing and contrasting children's development levels. Still, it's hard not to see the rampant success of skill building in the Montessori community.

Challenges Montessori Parents and Teachers Have Adjusting to New Skill Development Methods

We should spend at least a moment addressing the challenge that Montessori teachers and parents face. This is not the standard technique, and many adults have trouble allowing children to self-direct their early learning. The idea that reading, numerical sense, and language development can be self-taught or self-directed is foreign in our standard education system.

However, it is largely that predetermined or traditional education system causing these perception problems. Not only can children develop an interest in reading, language, and numbers on their own, but they can explore that interest avidly if they have the right tools. During Montessori observation, children may be better at directing the learning as they are naturally inclined to create games.

Learning number sense, learning to read, learning the alphabet, and learning to write can all be games present in the child's natural element.

Language and Speech Skills

Language and speech skills go back directly to the core of Montessori practice. A lot of the elements necessary to develop language and speech skills depend on classic Montessori tools. These tools can include sandpaper letters and phonetic letters or cards. Have the child lead and to offer Insight rather than correction. However, language is a particularly problematic subject within the English language.

English is a difficult language to tie directly to phonetic sounds. Much of our language has silent spellings and letters, which changes the core sound of the word away from its phonetic pronunciation. For example, "bear" does not sound like "b," "eh," ah," "rr," it sounds like "bare," and that's a different word. It seems like we're over-complicating the matter here, but giving children a real-life application of phonetics is simply done with sandpaper letters. Ask them to choose the letter that matches the sound you make.

Activity

Using sandpaper letters, read through a book, or go through a nursery rhyme. As you say a word or emphasize a sound, point to the letter that makes that same sound.

- "Ka" - C
- "Ba" - B
- "Da" - D

After you point it out to them for a while, your child will replicate your behavior. You may quickly notice they will happily lead this game on their own. They may even play it without you around, but giving them the basics or the fundamental elements is the jumping-off point they need.

What tools do you need for language and speech development? Try having these tools on hand:

- Moving alphabet
- Sandpaper letters
- Board books (your favorites are fine, embrace authors like Dr. Seuss or Eric Carle who evoke rhymes and repetition)
- Objects on flashcards or pictures on flashcards

Activity

A particularly fun activity is allowing the child to match an item to a picture card or flashcard. Give them a box or bucket of small items and a set of cards with things that match. A card with a ball, for example, would match the ball pit ball from the bucket. Your child can self-lead this activity. They may not start matching items, but give them some time, and they'll figure it out.

A variant of this activity provides them with a bucket of items and then use sandpaper letters. Then pick up an item. You can ask what sound matches this "Beee-ar" or "Zzzzebra"?

The first sound is important at first, but you can quickly revert to just saying the word how it comes naturally. Don't lead every activity like this, and you don't need to correct them if they say something a little off. If they're outright saying the wrong word, then feel free to say the correct word and show the correct movement to the sound.

Number Skills and Concept Development

Number skills actually come much more naturally to us than the traditional school system leads us to believe. It is through the rigidity of memorizing times tables and running mathematic drills that people feel they are inherently bad at math or that math is complex. In fact, number skills are some of the earliest skills we learn in terms of mental work. Not only can toddlers learn to count at a young age, but they also understand the value and comprehend the concepts of less and more.

These activities are engaging ways to get your child exercising their number sense without dragging them through a math lesson.

Activity

Snowflake cards are pretty easy to find, and you can easily make them yourself. Create or use cards with a few different snowflake designs, specifically those that have a different number of branches. Have two of each design.

Toddlers can match the cards or count the snowflake branches. After a while, you may notice your toddler arranging the cards in order from most to fewest branches or the other way around.

Activity

Deci-pockets are the open pocket tools that hang against the wall. Children or toddlers can handle their moving alphabet or moving numbers by moving them around on the wall within the deci-pocket.

For this activity, don't focus on getting the numbers in order straight away. Instead, focus on using the numbers to aid in nursery rhymes and small stories. You can use them to help your toddler follow along to rhymes such as, "5 little monkeys" or "5 little speckled frogs."

And you can use numbers in a story. You can make up stories, have your toddler make up stories, or simply go through your day. For example, you can start, "Today we woke up at eight," (then use the number eight in the deci-pocket) and follow up with, "*We will have a snack at ten.*" You can get elaborate by emphasizing the number of anything, really. "*You watched Tinkerbell and her five fairy friends.*" Or "*We bought one big jug of milk at the store.*"

Developing Writing Skills

Writing doesn't just include language. It also includes numbers. Some great Montessori tools come with developing writing skills, and they all are presented as games or fun activities.

There are activities to develop writing skills that happen both during the learning to write process and pre-writing. With pre-writing activities, you will focus on developing that pincer grip and hand movement. That often happens with wooden objects, stacking items, and nesting items.

To help develop a pincer grip, allow your child to use tweezers during sorting activities, or to hold standard size crayons or pencils. It may be easier for a toddler to handle egg-shaped crayons or oversized crayons, but using that standard size will help them build up the muscles they need to handle a pen or pencil appropriately.

The most notable writing tool from the Montessori method is salt writing or a salt tray. You can use the sandpaper letters, sandpaper numbers, or number and letter cutouts to help the child trace the shape with their finger. Then they make the same movement in the salt tray to write out the number or letter. You don't need a fancy tray or even fancy letter cutouts. You can do this activity on a budget, and if you haven't invested in sandpaper letters or numbers yet, you can simply write them out yourself and have your child trace over what you've written. The only thing to note here is that Himalayan salt or kosher salt does work better because the granules are not as fine, and they won't fall back into those holes as quickly. You can also use the same salt repeatedly. You are by no means wasting salt.

Finally, we will leave you with an activity that can grow with your child and helps the story building element of writing. Use either a chalkboard or dry erase board to encourage your child to explore writing independently. Most modern parents prefer dry erase boards to a chalkboard, but remember that chalkboards are harder to wipe away, and they may get a greater sense of reward from seeing their work remain in place rather than getting frustrated that the dry erases pen wipes away unintentionally.

They may not even use words for their writing. They may start storytelling with pictures. Don't worry because it is the same muscles holding that bit of chalk or that dry erase marker that they'll use to craft letters and numbers later in life. Storytelling is often neglected in traditional schools until they reach later grades. Instead, Kindergarten teachers and first-grade teachers often provide stories rather than engage the child in story building. By allowing your child to create a story through pictures or words on a chalkboard or a dry erase board, you develop two skills at once. Plus, storytelling is an engaging way to keep your child interested in writing and pursuing that interest.

Activities can help cultivate an interest in a numerical sense, reading, and writing. It is important to acknowledge that unlike traditional schools, Montessori children often learn to write and read when they're learning their alphabet and numbers. Instead of staggering the learning stage from learning the alphabet to the reading and writing alphabet, the learning process is ongoing. It may seem as though toddlers are taking longer to pick up on the alphabet or numbers if they're also learning to read and write them. However, you will reach a point where everything clicks into place.

Using all three activities at once, learning to read, write, and use number sense also allows your child to utilize their short attention span. This isn't something that most parents get to cash in on often, but toddlers have a short attention span. Don't try to sit your toddler down and teach them to write for 30-minutes straight. Instead, use fun activities to engage in writing, reading, and numerical learning. That way, they can jump from activity to activity, and they don't even realize that they're learning and developing the same skill.

Chapter 10: Interesting Arts and Crafts for Creative Toddler

By and large, the Montessori method engages children in a way that promotes creativity. Developing creativity at such a young age has drastically changed the lives of many who grew up with early Montessori education, even if they entered into traditional or standard education systems afterward. Creativity lends itself to our ability to think analytically and dive into problem-solving.

Without creativity, we cannot analyze data. We cannot construct or build structures. We could not solve the problems of the world. Although that seems like a scaling way out of proportion for toddlers, it comes down to just that. Creative kids become our strategic problem solvers. We've acknowledged in other chapters some all-stars from Montessori education, and among them is Will Wright. The creator of the Sims produced, built, and continues to generate something that the video game industry had not seen before. He offered a solution to the violent video game or story-driven video game culture. He presented a sandbox world for people to explore through an avatar of their own creation.

Now, where does creativity start? With the Montessori environment, there should be a variety of creative tools and outlets for the child. Toddlers are naturally creative, possibly because they don't have preconceived notions about how certain things should work. They don't pick up a crayon and think, "Oh, I need a piece of paper," they turn right to the wall and get busy. In this chapter, we look at specific arts and crafts that toddlers excel at, and we address the tools you need for these activities.

Arts and Crafts Build Imagination and More

Arts and crafts build imagination, creativity, self-confidence, boost self-exploration, but they also offer a lot of tangible or practical skills. While some parents encourage children to seek creative efforts for the sake of their imagination and creativity, others are more worried about real-world elements. Don't worry; if you're a parent who is more concerned about mathematics and science, you're not alone. But art and math aren't so different.

There are basic rules that come with art, and your child will learn those naturally. There are life skills that come with crafting. In fact, handicrafts play a role in systems such as the Girl Scouts and the Boy Scouts of America because they develop life skills and self-confidence.

Things to Keep in Mind

There are few things to remember when introducing Arts, crafts, and new activities involving creativity to your child. First, the material should always be accessible or at your toddler's height.

You might have some initial concern that your toddler has access to their crayons at all times without supervision, but there are ways to get around that concern. You can always choose washable or mess-free paint, crayons, and markers. And Crayola has a Color Wonder line that only works when the pens or paint contact special paper. This is excellent for parents that want the materials to be available all the time, but also don't want it all over the walls or floor.

The second thing to remember is the quality of the materials. Have you ever tried to color with half-melted crayons? While it isn't impossible and we should expect our children to develop resourcefulness, if you start with high-quality materials, they will last longer, and will be more enjoyable to work with. Toddlers are easily frustrated, and if they get frustrated every time they go to their crayon box or paint, they will just stop interacting with those items. Toddlers are masters of avoidance for managing frustration.

Finally, one of the most important elements to consider when putting together craft kits or material for a toddler is that less is more. One of the recurring lessons in the Montessori method is that we should not over-stimulate the children or provide too many options. You don't need a pocket watch with every color under the sun. Fewer supplies provide greater exploration because it relies on natural resourcefulness.

But wait, what about those great painters that have bottles and bottles and bottles of different colors? To give some context, the well-known painter Bob Ross works with only 13 colors. Every one of Ross's paintings relied on 13 foundational colors, and he mixed them as he painted. Toddlers don't need all 13 of those colors. It's a little comical to think I'm handing Alizarin Crimson to a two-year-old. You can actually start with just the primary colors. Red, yellow, and blue can easily mix to create a wide variety of painting options.

With crayons and markers, you might branch out into a 7 or 10 pack where they can have access to a wider variety but are still not overwhelmed with the options.

Don't discourage your child from using household items. If your toddler decides that a paper towel is better than copy paper or brown paper, then let it happen. Maybe the texture of the paper towels enticed them to try something new. It's these little moments of creative thinking that you don't want to put down.

Activities

So, what activities can your toddler do? Like most other sections of this book, thinking about your toddler's restrictions is slightly off the mark because the realm of creativity and crafting is almost endless. We have a collection of activities here that can get you started, but feel free to engage your own creativity and explore with your child how many arts and crafts options are really in your home. It's a fun way to connect with your kids.

Clip and Cut Activity

Depending on where you stand, the clip and cut activity could be one of the best or the worst parenting tips you've heard. In Montessori, children are given tools that are safe but do require supervision. The clip and cut activity is not something that you will leave your child alone with; this is a great activity for an observation period where you are sitting nearby and watching closely.

Hand your toddler a pair of kid-safe scissors and a stack of construction paper. They will figure out what to do quickly, although they do try to cut their hair. With your kid clipping away at construction paper, they're developing a pincer grip, but they're also creating shapes. If you start with a square piece or rectangular piece of construction paper, anything they cut out of that is a shape.

They are unknowingly creating triangles, circles, rectangles, rhombuses, and more. What happens with the clip and cut activity? Because it is largely self-led, they will find innate ways to pick up on these shapes. They don't have a name to give these shapes yet, and they don't realize there are proper ways to create a shape. They are taking raw activity and slowly refining it. For the clip and cut activity, the toddler will soon realize that some consistent shapes are arising from their activity, and then they will try to recreate those shapes again and again. Over just a few weeks, you might notice that your child went from slashing at the sides of the paper to cutting out a diamond shape carefully.

Unconventional Paintbrushes Activity

By the age of two or three, your child has probably had some experience with paintbrushes, and it can be fun to change the tool. This is one creative activity that builds those problem-solving muscles in the brain. Imagine if you went to write a letter and had no pen or pencil? What would you do? That is what you're proposing to your child.

Similar to many other activities throughout this book, this activity is self-led. Prevent your child from using their paint, a piece of paper, or canvas, and instead of offering paintbrushes, provide pompoms, small squares of felt, twisted up pipe cleaners, and even crumpled plastic wrap. How long does it take before they experiment with the different results from each new painting tool? Do they have a favorite they seem to prefer? You can mix this up by swapping out paintbrushes about halfway through the activity. If your child seems to lose steam, offer a paintbrush and see if they prefer it over the alternative tools you've offered.

Mosaic Paper Punches Activity

If you have a handful of construction paper on hand, then you can grab a good old-fashioned hole punch and go to town. If you have specialized hole punches, you can provide larger circles or different shapes. In traditional schools, this lines up with a similar activity meant for middle schoolers where they use small hole punches to make many tiny circles and then use those to cover an existing picture.

In this activity, you will provide your toddler with the hole punch of remnants, the tiny little circles, and a blank piece of paper. Slightly sticky paper works excellently. However, you can also take a glue stick and liberally apply it to the paper so anything that falls on it will stick.

The toddlers can apply the hole punch remnants to the paper, stack them, throw them like confetti, it doesn't matter. Overtime, however, they'll see these small dots can come together to make a picture. Similar to Monet, you're encouraging your child to use an unexpected shape to create larger images.

If you're worried about the size of the hole punch remnants, you can fold over a piece of construction paper multiple times and then cut a single circle and have much larger circles for your toddler to use. With effort on the part of the adults, either way will probably result in a hand cramp. Some parents have turned to simply ordering stickers. Ordering circular stickers are not cheating, it just provides a sticky backing for basically the same size circle.

Play-Dough Activities

When talking about Montessori, we're rarely inclined to jump into corporate names such as Play-Doh. However, this activity boosts Sensorial development, creative play, and can even prolong their attention span because of how open-ended this activity is. Now you can make play-dough at home! Do not go out and buy Play-Doh; the Play-Doh you make at home might even last longer.

To make your own Play-Doh, mix two cups of flour, 3/4 cup of salt, four teaspoons of cream of tartar, two cups of Warm Water, two tablespoons of oil, and food coloring. You can mix all the ingredients except for the food coloring and then divide them into separate sandwich bags and color them that way.

Then hand the super soft and squishy play-dough to your kid on a cookie sheet. They can do whatever they want with this crafting material. They can wrap it around items. They can use stamps to stamp different shapes into place, or even use cookie cutters to cut out shapes.

Spaghetti Activities

There is a reason so many parents love doing crafts that involve spaghetti. First, it's cheap. Second, it's easy to put together; you just throw in some boiling water, and finally, it works so many muscles and skills. Wet spaghetti is difficult to hold on to, and it's slimy. By using cooked spaghetti for different crafts and activities, you can build up those fine muscles skills in your toddler's hands, boost their sensory exposure, and help them exercise their creativity.

What first? Your toddler can paint with spaghetti. Boil up some spaghetti and then put the spaghetti right into the paint. They can pick up a noodle and smear it across the paper or wax paper and create many designs that they probably couldn't achieve with paintbrushes. Alternatively, you can boil the spaghetti, coat it in margarine or butter, so it hardens up, and let it dry. Then, let your toddler lay out the cold noodles onto the paper, and paint over them with foam-tipped paintbrushes. Not only is this activity fun, but it is a lot less messy than you might expect from painting with pasta.

The next spaghetti activity can be used to make a wind chime, dreamcatcher, and really a wide variety of other shapes and figures as well. For example, while this started as an early activity for one little girl, Bella, with making a dreamcatcher, it turned into a winter activity and making snowflakes. Have your child dry spaghetti noodles and if they can handle it, a bit of glue, or play-dough that you don't mind drying out.

Then they can use the dry spaghetti noodles by snapping them into different lengths and sticking them with glue or play-dough to create a dreamcatcher, snowflakes, spider webs, and much more.

These activities are all meant to boost creativity, so do your best not to interject while the child is engaging in these activities. You might feel inclined to acknowledge that the paintbrush doesn't work that way, or the Play-Doh isn't meant for that. But honestly, there are so many uses available through arts and crafts materials that our toddlers may even teach us new and exciting ways to use the same old tools.

Chapter 11: Positive Discipline in the Montessori Home

Discipline is one of the most widely covered and controversial topics that appear in parenting books, on blogs, and in various other mediums. Social media is brimming with judgmental parents and non-parents who feel compelled to give their advice and insight. Try to bring in a judge-free mentality for this chapter because the Montessori discipline does spark a lot of controversies. Not only that, it preaches self-discipline, but it also preaches positive discipline and not encouraging your child.

Now, self-discipline is something we're all familiar with and is really something we expand on as adults. We learn the hard way we are responsible for our behavior, our reactions, and other elements of our life that until adulthood seem out of our control. Self-discipline, or the lack of it, is largely to blame for much of that teenage angst.

Diving into the positive discipline and the controversial element of encouraging your child or offering praise, it will take more than the brief touch on self-discipline. In this chapter, you'll find a variety of techniques largely regarded as positive discipline and have been found to build empathy and a cooperative relationship. The

Montessori method is not the only system or belief pattern that offers positive discipline. Many pediatricians and child psychiatrists also support Maria Montessori's foundation for positive discipline. It's worth noting now; positive discipline sounds a little backward. Most of us were raised with good old traditional negative discipline, which is as bad as it sounds. Both parents not only believe that that's normal but don't know how else to approach discipline. It's not just spanking or going into a timeout. Negative discipline can also come in the form of how to talk to our children and how we behave when they don't act the way we want.

Through this chapter, we hope to give you the information, tools, and resources necessary for you to understand positive discipline and how to build self-discipline within your child.

We completely understand that every parent has a different approach to parenting. We hope that you'll consider promoting self-discipline and using the tools for positive discipline.

Be Proactive - The Foundation for Positive Discipline

One of the most highly commended personal development books is The 7 Habits of Highly Effective People. On its own, the book offers insight and advice beyond value for any adult, but, as a parent, it's worth coming back to that first habit of 'being proactive.' Being proactive establishes a level of fairness in the household when it comes to living with or engaging with a toddler. Toddlers may not know much about rules and may have little respect for authority in any capacity, but they understand fairness.

So how can you be proactive and build a foundation for positive discipline?

Make very clear rules that can't fall into any other interpretation. Toddlers and young children especially like to push boundaries, and if there's an opportunity to misinterpret a rule, they'll take it. So, make very clear, understandable, and consistent rules.

Examples of these can include:

- Only nice touching
- No biting people
- No hitting
- No slapping
- No kicking people or animals
- Clean up before starting a new activity

Ideally, these rules won't include the word "*no*" or "*don't*," but there are only so many ways to phrase restriction on your toddler's freedom. Freedom with restrictions is the overarching concept within the Montessori method, and you're allowing your toddler a lot of freedom, but there are restrictions. Your toddler should not inflict physical harm on you or any other living creature. Your child will eventually have to learn to clean up and all variety of other life skills.

The trick to establishing a foundation has a few core rules; ones you can always revert back to, which is why rules such as "Only nice touching," work so well. When a child does something, you have to survey only whether that was nice touching or not nice touching (kicking, biting, and so forth).

The other way that you will work proactively to build a foundation of positive discipline is to cultivate a worry-free environment. You've already read the chapter on creating the Montessori environment, and we look at how eliminating likely dangers but promoting interest and engagement can help deter a lot of the times that parents have to tell their child to stop doing something. Essentially, eliminating the number of times you have to step into discipline will make your discipline efforts more effective. If your toddler is told "*no*" 50 times a day, any one of those times won't stand out more than the other 49 times they were told the word "*no*." However, if you have to say "*no*" on a rare occasion, then it is impactful.

What is Self-Discipline?

The holy grail of most productive and happy adults is that they aren't overwhelmed and overstressed Type-A people. Self-discipline is the ability and the willingness of a person to monitor and correct their own behavior. This is something that we have to learn, and it's something that our children must learn. It's not a natural feature for most people. It is also often mis-attributed to willpower. Self-discipline and willpower are different things. You need not teach your child to abstain or persevere for the sake of willpower training.

So, how do you teach toddler self-discipline? Unfortunately, the best way to do it is to start removing or pulling back on things that we've enjoyed doing as parents: praise and reward. When children are told not to do something, and they face punishment, they only know not to do the thing because there's a punishment waiting. As with most things in life, the opposite is as true of this initial statement. When children are told to do something, and they know there's a reward, they only do it because of the reward.

Children and toddlers build self-discipline by learning the value of doing what's right and receiving the intrinsic reward of a job well done. Eventually, your child will take their dishes to the sink, not because you told them to and then thanked them afterward, but because they know that that is the right thing to do after they finish their plate. Eventually, your toddler will know to apologize after pushing down another kid unintentionally, because it's the right thing to do. Toddlers build self-discipline through these many small acts, acknowledging when they were at fault or acting without prompting from a reward or a punishment.

A note on discipline: parents all have different ways of disciplining, but there are differences between discipline and punishment. Punishing is what it sounds like, punishing a child for unwanted behavior. Whereas discipline is upholding established rules and standards. You'll use kindness and firmness to promote self-respect, self-discipline, cooperation, problem-solving, and desired behavior. Now, it is still frustrating. A screaming toddler is a screaming toddler, and sometimes mommy or daddy need a break.

But, over time, teaching or promoting self-discipline will make day-to-day life much easier.

How can you build self-discipline?

- Pull back on your praise - say thank you only when appropriate and give very specific compliments.
- E.g., Instead of, "*You're so smart,*" use, "*You figured that out, can you show me how you did it?*"
- Show interest in your child's activities without telling them they're the best thing since sliced cheese - watch them, be present, and engage in the activity with them when invited. It means more than a passive compliment.
- Provide the opportunity to make meaningful choices.
- When faced with undesired behavior, try your best not to acknowledge it or excuse yourself.
- Have high expectations.
- Say "*yes*" more often than "*no.*"
- Give simple and clear directions.
- Repeat expected rules often.

When put together, these small actions or mild changes and how you interact with your toddler can have a big impact on their self-discipline.

Elements of Positive Discipline

The key elements of positive discipline revolve around responsibility, cooperation, objective thinking, respect, courtesy, honesty, and compassion. Wouldn't we all love for our toddlers to understand and employ these elements often?

But a toddler's decision-making center of the brain simply isn't developed enough to acknowledge and act in line with these elements, all the time. The best you can do to put these positive elements into play in your household is to model those behaviors. Now, you might do that already, but your child doesn't know that. Your child doesn't have a name to give these actions, and they can't identify those actions in the moment. When do you notice there is a decision regarding responsibility, respect, honesty, or courtesy, point it out to your toddler. It can feel very self-absorbed at first, but by saying, "*I opened the door for someone because it was polite,*" you're calling attention to that very specific action. Another example might be saying, "*Dad works with your sister during playtime, and that's why they have so much fun. They cooperate.*"

What Happens When Children Break the Rules?

Safety is always paramount, and sometimes, you can't talk your way through rule-breaking. This goes beyond the tantrums and bleeds into running into the street, or not holding hands in a parking lot. And there's another issue with getting out of their car seat. Those snazzy busy boards help kids learn how to open snaps and clips, making them car seat Houdinis.

When a child breaks the rules, there are a few ways to handle it. If safety is a factor, then removing them from the situation is often the best initial response. There is also the option of further restrictions on freedom. For example, if your child is constantly escaping their car seat, it may not be safe to take them out as often as you might have because they've shown there's a clear pattern they won't stay in their car seat when they need to for safety reasons. If they miss grocery trips, you might notice your toddler asking to go out with you, and then you can emphasize that they can go with you if they stay in their car seat. If they refuse to stay in their seat again, then you may choose not to take them out without help from another adult.

Biting, Scratching, Hair Pulling, and Other Physical Attacks

These issues are not as much of an emergency as they initially seem. It's developmentally appropriate. Your kid is not a bad kid, and the best approach is through proactive play. You can role-play with stuffed animals, where one stuffed animal gets hit, and the other animal says I don't like that and leaves. This is one of the few directed Montessori activities because it directly addresses how it is appropriate and respectful to touch or engage another person.

When it's directed toward you, stop their hands or feet, and say something like, "*I won't let you hit me.*" And emphasize that hitting/kicking hurt. One of the few times that Montessori aligns with outside teaching is in these moments. Positive parenting comes from a lesson seen in the <u>Happiest Toddler on the Block</u> and focuses on Kind Ignoring.

Kind ignoring is the act of removing yourself from the situation. Now, you don't want to shame or put down the child, but acknowledge that the behavior is not okay, it hurts, and you don't want it to happen to you. Acknowledge also that you will be back or available later.

- Try these:

- "*Mom doesn't like slaps. Mom will be back when you stop slapping.*"

- *"Dad doesn't like bites. They hurt. Dad wants alone time because these bites hurt."*

- *"I don't like hits; they feel bad. I'll come back in a bit when you don't feel like hitting anymore."*

These emphasize responsibility on their part and aren't a punishment, although your toddler won't feel that way. You have removed yourself from physical pain. That's not a punishment for your child, it's a relief for you. Now when you leave your child's area or room, just be sure that it's a safe place for them. If you've Montessori-styled your home, then you shouldn't have to worry about that.

Kind ignoring is also the go-to option for tantrums you can't talk through. In an ideal situation with positive discipline, you'll be able to sit down and discuss what happened when your child started their tantrum. Always intervene early before the tantrum gets out of hand.

You can acknowledge what they want or the things they can't find, but sometimes tantrums are just too emotional to reel in. Your toddler is an emotional being, and you have decades of logical thinking. The two don't align often. If you're getting frustrated, or you feel that you're tending toward negative discipline or physical punishment, kind ignoring can give you a break and a moment to decompress. Then you can get back into having that conversation with your toddler and de-escalate their fit.

Regarding Sharing

Montessori encourages more adult methods of sharing, which is complex because many Montessori teachers simply say they don't teach sharing. The model of sharing isn't that "everything is yours for the taking," which often adults jump in to present when they see children not sharing. Instead, Montessori emphasizes turn-taking. You are sharing the item, and that doesn't mean the child is forfeiting their time with the item simply because another child became interested in it. The second child can wait patiently until the first child has moved on.

Now, in public situations, sharing can get much more complex. You might encourage your child to learn specific words such as "turn," or "wait," to help them express they are not done with the toy yet. Particularly during toddler years, you'll have trouble because toddlers like to play next to each other but not necessarily with each other.

Whether you promote turn-taking over traditionally modeled toddler sharing where whoever had it first needs to give it up, or whoever had it first keeps the toy, is up to you.

Special Note for the Parents

Parenting is hard. Toddlers are prone to emotional outbursts, tantrums, and screaming fits for what seems like no reason. If committing to Montessori positive discipline sounds difficult, remember that you will still deal with tantrums, sharing problems, and outbursts no matter what discipline method you use. What it comes down to is which discipline method works best for you, and how that disciplined method impacts your relationship with the child.

With Montessori learning and encouragement, traditional discipline doesn't promote the level of independence that Montessori teaching does. Now your child is looking for a rule rather than looking at you to model your behavior. If a child encounters a new situation, they do what they want and suffer the consequences later. Whereas self-discipline and positive discipline help the child make more conscientious choices earlier.

Chapter 12: Growing Montessori

Toddlers don't just grow; they grow fast. You don't have to talk to an early childhood development specialist or psychiatrist to know that from day-to-day, week-to-week, and month-to-month, your toddler is quickly evolving into an different person. They do have core elements of their personality as a foundation. Still, they're learning at such a fast rate that not surprisingly, as adults we are so surprised at how quickly they move from one interest to another or from one challenge to another. Taking off shoes can be an impossible task one day, and easy-breezy the next.

So, one of the common questions that come up with Montessori in the home is how to accommodate such a fast-growing tiny person. Your toddler will inevitably grow and go through changes, both physically and mentally. You can apply the Montessori method to help acknowledge these changes. You can address topics such as clinginess, separation anxiety, tantrums, teething, potty training, and more.

We know that using the toddler Montessori discipline is only one step in your parental journey. We didn't want to leave you without all the information you might need to keep moving forward down this path with the Montessori method in mind. As you employ the Montessori method with your toddler, a lot of the principles and foundational elements will become second nature. It can become easy to find times to observe, guide, and understand exactly how your child is trying to communicate. That gives you more license to advance in Montessori and guide your child through that process as you improve.

Key Times in Physical Development Happen in the Early Years

The key moments in physical development throughout the early years include teething, learning to pull themselves up, learning to crawl, learning to walk, learning to open and shut items, and more. Even at the toddler age, it may seem as though your child has hit the major physical development milestones. However, your toddler is still growing. Their perception is physically changing as they grow taller and build upon smaller physical development milestones.

The milestones many people overlook or simply don't know how to address during toddler years include developing the pincer grip, learning how to hold a crayon or pencil, operating scissors, and more fine-tuned movements.

Remember that most successful students have begun complex stringed instruments as young as three or four years old. Those instruments are demanding with finger movement and fine motor skills.

Toddlers are still developing their larger motor functions, most toddlers don't jump proficiently until about two and half years old, and many may have a slightly wonky run until they're about three or four.

While it is fun to have this information on hand, through Montessori guidance, it's also beneficial to know in terms of presenting activities. If you notice that your child can proficiently jump, then you can encourage more outdoor activity that require jumping or leaping. And if you notice that your child has no problem handling small objects with their hands, you might introduce a new instrument or new tools that require more delicate precision with handwork.

Growing Up Challenges

With the challenges of growing, especially at the rate that toddler's do, it's good to have a well-stocked tool belt for handling these issues. What is the Montessori method? We know that redirection is an powerful tool. Along with redirection, you can also encourage toddlers to play and you can provide engaging independent activities. The combination of these three can help address issues such as clinginess and separation anxiety.

If you have stopped by a Montessori School, you may have already seen this in action. Often when parents approach the new student, the Montessori teacher will take the child and guide them to nearby activities so the parent can leave after they've said goodbye. It drastically reduces the outbursts and creates a positive experience for the child. Now, when you're using Montessori at home, this may seem more of a challenge. You may need to take the initiative and have the other adult redirect attention so you can step away.

Clinginess and separation anxiety is an common challenge for toddlers. Most have spent more time with one parent than anyone else that they know. It can also seem as though that parent is leaving and will never come back.

Toddlers don't need a history of abandonment to have this worry that someone will not return. Some have not developed that understanding that things or people leave and come back. Saying goodbye peacefully and then redirecting your attention can be the key to reducing separation anxiety and clinginess. The Montessori method largely promotes the development of independence, especially from an early age.

As you promote that independence, the toddler may lapse into extreme clinginess. It is a common cause of backsliding. To help continue forward motion in building independence, you can establish "independent times" where you sit back and observe. During these times, you're not available for together play or providing help with challenges or struggles they can handle on their own. Independent time is actually a great opportunity for completely absent observation. Redirect their attention, let them know that you'll be back shortly, and then find a spot out of eyesight. If you notice your child needs help, use this as an opportunity to observe how they overcome the challenge.

For toilet training, potty training, or bathroom learning, this can be a particular challenge. You'll need a potty or seat for your toilet and then walk them through the potty process.

Toys that Grow with Them

Most of the Montessori tools are already meant to grow with your children. If they were in a Montessori School, you might notice that six and seven-year-olds are still playing with the Pink Tower and building blocks. With the modern age, most parents accept or believe that children tire of toys quickly and need new materials to remain engaged. While toddlers can become tired of seeing the same thing again and again, the idea with some of these toys is that you modify how you play with them. Then some toys may follow them even into teenage years and adulthood if the interest is developed and continued.

Let's tackle adjustable furniture first. What's the Montessori prepared environment, toddlers should have toddler size furniture. However, with adaptable cribs and toddler beds, you can invest in one piece of furniture that can grow with your child. The same is possible with moving from a highchair to a booster seat, to removing the seat all together for sitting at the table. A toddler seat or couch may simply enter retirement after the child has outgrown it. Some furniture type materials such as art easels are usually adjustable.

When looking at musical tools, you might have to pay special attention to instruments that don't require scaling. We're not talking about musical scales. We're talking about size. You simply cannot purchase an adult violin and expect a four-year-old to handle it well. You would need a smaller, or to-scale, violin.

However, we don't scale down pianos or drums. There are "kid" versions of these, which use cheaper materials and aren't built to last. But a four-year-old can learn piano on a full-size piano. A child can learn to drum on full-size drum sets. If you are looking to invest in instruments, then you might prioritize instruments that won't need full replacement every other year.

Water play can also grow with your child. While they may show a special interest in plungers, pictures, and even water wheels for pouring in their early years, they may enjoy more advanced activities as we approach the ages of five or six. Allowing them to construct waterways or direct water traffic can be an exciting way to change a water pouring station. Water is enjoyable at almost any age, and it comes with unmatched benefits in terms of learning the water cycle and the basics of physics. Our world largely functions on water, and keeping that interest peaked at a young age can help them understand its role in our world later in life.

Blocks and stacking blocks are another big-ticket item that can grow with your child. Even at the ages of 11 or 12, blocks can be a part of everyday play. Your toddler may have simply stacked up a tower and then knocked it over. Now, older children might build castles, create bridges, or even create designs and shapes that are unique but recognizable.

One of the common questions that parents of growing children ask about Montessori involves play. The question is usually, is doll play considered Montessori learning? Now, dolls and dollhouses rarely have a place in Montessori schools. Because of the importance and focus given to the scientific method, these creative or open-ended play are often left to the home environment. There is nothing that would allude to Maria Montessori being against doll play. In fact, many children use dolls for reenacting everyday situations and use them to explore conversation and interaction. All of those elements are present in the majority of Montessori activities. It seems a little ridiculous, but generally, you would aim toward a less guided play environment. What we're getting down to is that dolls, dollhouses, cars, and furniture are just fine. They're actually great because of how long children will play with dolls throughout their childhood and even into early adolescence. However, you might choose a doll with a house rather than a doll and a doctor's coat with a doctor's office. Allow your child to recreate those things using materials they have at home, let them bring creativity to doll play rather than relying on preconceived environments.

Parenting Habits Change and Adapt

As a toddler goes through tantrums and potty training, two of the most common challenges for parents, you can change and adapt your habits to promote development. Many parents cite that potty training is one of the keystones in developing conversations. You not only have to address the function of the toilet and the necessity of potty training, but also addressing concerns and fears that the toddler has associated with potty training.

Have Conversations

The famous book entitled <u>The Montessori Toddler</u>, from Simone Davis, covered a specific challenge in allowing your toddler to have a tantrum. It encouraged parents to acknowledge the child's feelings and walk them through processing those feelings. Not every parent is prepared to do this in every environment that toddlers have tantrums. In fact, most publications that cover this particular element from this book don't cite the most problematic times that toddlers have tantrums. However, there's a bit of a twist. When you use this method ahead of time, it becomes a proactive way of developing conversations that are effective and fast. When a growing toddler or child is having a tantrum at home, you can take your time to walk them through exactly what's happening. But also do this when they're not having tantrums. After your toddler becomes a child, they are taking one more step toward adulthood, and what they need from you is a conversation. They don't need a pandering voice saying, "*Oh, I understand that you are sad.*" They need someone who's going to talk to them like a person.

When your toddler has that tantrum, or has to face that fear of the potty, or is having trouble sleeping on their own after so many years of the family bed, that is the time to have the hard conversations. Then, when your toddler goes into tantrum mode in a grocery store, you can have that fast and efficient conversation to wrap it up quickly and get on with your shopping.

There is a hard to identify moment in development where children go from needing you to mimic what's happening, to you setting the tone for the conversation that's happening. Earlier in this book, we cited mimicking tantrums and repeating what your toddler was saying. Now, when your child can communicate what they want, or it's clear that they feel the situation is unjust or targeted against them, you can engage in a different type of conversation. You can start with that original mimicking. You can say something like, "Reina, you are so mad that he has candy, and I'm not letting you have any." with the statement, you are acknowledging their feelings and site the core of the tantrum. They saw another kid with candy, they asked you for candy, you told them no, end of the story. Now, for the sake of consistency and maintaining a respectful relationship between your decision-making and their existence in the world, you can't give in to their demands for candy every time. You can, however, have a conversation.

Patience Stretching

With tantrums, listening skills, and continuing development through childhood years, your kid needs some patience. Patience is a vital life skill, but it also helps to deter tantrums and increase listening skills. Patience stretching is one of the guided elements of Montessori, and it spreads to many other methods of positive discipline.

When your kid has a tantrum, or even a toddler starts to throw a tantrum, get them to scale it down by counting. This is mildly redirecting their attention. You aren't setting them on a completely different course; you are putting the tantrum on pause. You can count to three, five, or even ten, and when you see that their breathing has started to calm down, you can begin the patience stretching.

To exercise patience stretching, get the toddler to count to 10 calmly. You can start first, take a deep breath and say "*one*," and wait for them to repeat. Then when you get to 10, you can say, "*Okay, now ask me nicely.*" Usually, this works, but do this when there aren't tantrums happening.

You can build this skill by using patient stretching and everyday activities. If your child is stacking blocks, then ask them to count with you before stacking the next block. You can also do this when you're getting ready to sit down and eat. Patience stretching is not a reward. There will be plenty of times you will need to rely on patience stretching just to calm down a tantrum, and even then, the child may not get their way.

As your child grows, you'll see the benefits of patient stretching, having conversations, and having tools that grow with your child. Not only will it foster greater independence, but you'll can see them adapt to their changing environment. The Montessori method is not just for early childhood development; it can follow them well into their teenage years and even adulthood.

Conclusion

Thank you for reading, and we hope that you've found all the resources necessary to get started with Montessori learning for your child. Toddlers are a challenge, but with the Montessori method, you can spend time watching them with a new fascination for how their tiny minds work and develop. Use the Montessori discipline for toddlers to help build up the creative thinking, language, mathematics, coordination, and problem-solving abilities of your child.

Through these activities, you can support creativity and engage their minds in new and unexpected ways. Get them up and moving with music and movement, or have their little fingers hard at work, sorting out differently colored objects. These activities are fun for toddlers, and, usually, they're pretty easy for the adults to set up and monitor.

Start by creating the right environment for Montessori engagement by thoughtfully placing toys and other objects. Then move on to presenting activities that are age appropriate but still present a challenge. Finally, keep growing by encouraging further sensory and coordination development along with those smarts your child is already showing!

Part 2: Toddler Sleep Training

The Ultimate Guide to Getting Your Children to Fall Asleep Fast and Sleep Through the Night

Introduction

Do you have a toddler whose sleeping habits continue to wear you out? If you answered "Yes" to that question, please know that you are not alone. Many parents have experienced the same problem and are aware of how exhausting and challenging it can be. In fact, it is one of the most challenging experiences that most parents have to handle, whether they are first-time parents or not.

Friends and family may have tried consoling you by telling you that this experience will pass. However, when exactly will that happen? Even if your toddler slept well when they were still an infant, toddlerhood might be a challenge since they will most likely be at a stage when their energy is at an all-time high. With that said, expect sleep to be the last thing they will want to do when it's bedtime.

Fortunately, there are ways to train your toddler to sleep, and this book will serve as your guide to help you apply those methods. This toddler sleep-training book is different from others you may have read. It contains useful tips and techniques that your child is likely to respond positively to as well.

Most of the sleep-training tips you will learn are up to date, so they will certainly work in these modern times. They are easy to follow and understand, so you can start using them immediately to train your toddler(s) to have happy dreams through the night. This book also uses tips specifically designed for toddlers and kids, so expect positive responses quickly.

Chapter 1: The Non-Sleepy Toddler: A Cause for Concern?

A familiar scenario among parents, whether they are first-timers or not, is having a smooth-sailing parenting experience once their babies overcome their sleeping difficulties and adapt better nighttime habits. The trouble is, they then end up being haunted by yet another challenge that affects their baby's sleep upon reaching toddlerhood.

Do you have the same problem? If so, it could be because of sleep regression, which often happens once babies are two years old, but sometimes as early as eighteen months. Your experience may be good overall before that stage. While it is true you may still have experienced instances when your child did not sleep well—because of teething or a medical issue—their sleeping habits were still good most nights.

Now that your toddler has reached the age when sleep regression often kicks in, things become more challenging and difficult for you. You will likely be exhausted from tending to their needs every time they decide they do not want to sleep.

Aside from the fatigue and its possible effects on your mood and overall health, many parents worry about their toddler's health and welfare. You may be worried about whether their inability to sleep will take a toll on their wellbeing. So, what really happens if your toddler cannot go to sleep? Should their sleep regression be a cause for concern? Is it time to visit their pediatrician or other medical specialists? Time to find out.

Sleep Regression and What to Expect When It Happens

Sleep regression is a scenario that occurs when your baby or toddler, who has had good sleeping patterns in the past, begins to wake up—often at night (in worse cases, they wakes up every twenty minutes) or displays behaviors that may have a negative impact on their sleep. These include taking shorter naps than usual or skipping them altogether for no clear reason. This regression may occur for a specific period—around three to six weeks in most cases.

If you are already used to putting your toddler to sleep without difficulty, this new scenario may take you off guard. You will most likely feel frustrated, not knowing what to do and how you can make them complete the required number of hours of sleep they need every day.

Your frustration will probably grow when you notice their inadequate sleep affecting several aspects of their growth and development. The sleep deprivation of both parents and toddler can also make your parenting tasks more difficult to fulfill. Aside from that, you may notice your toddler exhibiting temper tantrums and defiant and oppositional behavior. Why? The answer is because it is the natural result of sleep deprivation.

Imagine those scenarios if you have not experienced them yet, and you will most likely cringe at the thought of having to deal with such issues any time soon. Your child's defiant behavior may add to the fatigue and exhaustion you may have already felt. The even bigger problem is that both elements—their newfound sleeplessness and defiance—may likewise begin to influence each other.

You will notice them starting to refuse your requests, refuse taking naps, or stubbornly shouting or crying incessantly every time their sleep is disrupted at night. The insufficient sleep brought on by your toddler's sleep regression can also cause them to become crankier, eventually resulting in temper tantrums. Be aware that all the symptoms will reveal themselves and you will notice.

Those are just a few of the common scenarios that might happen when your toddler cannot get enough sleep. One way to combat those unwanted instances is to learn as much as you can about sleep regression. It would be best to familiarize yourself with the specific stages in your child's life when this is most likely to happen.

Knowing when to expect it, you can prepare yourself and set up techniques that will help you both handle the situation. Also, keep in mind that each baby or toddler is different. This means that your toddler's sleep regression signs may differ from the behaviors of others.

Though, in most cases, babies or toddlers undergo sleep regression during the following ages:

- **Four months** - The four-month sleep regression is indeed one of the most difficult stages in a parent's life. Most parents dread this specific stage as it is usually the first time their child's sleeping patterns are disrupted.

If your baby deals with sleep regression at this age, remember there are logical reasons for it. The most common reasons why your baby starts to show sleep problems are hunger caused by a growth spurt, the pain brought on by teething, and the fun and excitement they may feel as they learn to roll over.

- **Six months** – Sleep regression may also happen during your baby's sixth month. It is mainly because of the growth spurt they will most likely experience during this time, but take note: This is also the time when babies are already capable of sleeping through the night.

Most of them will just wake up for simple cuddles. As far as that is concerned, it would be best if you test a certain technique to train them to sleep well during this stage so that you will have a lower chance of dealing with the negative effects of sleep regression in the future. Small adjustments make all the difference, so try different techniques to make your baby feel secure.

- **Eight months** – This could go on until your child is up to ten months old. Note that this is the specific period when your baby will start to crawl. At around ten months, they may also start to stand up on their own. These new skills might disrupt their sleeping patterns. It would also be normal for babies to deal with separation anxiety during this stage. It might lead to them waking up at night, as they will seek your reassurance.

- **12 months** – Sleep regression during this age may be brought on by the new skills that your baby has started to acquire. It could be as simple as learning to stand up or taking their first steps. These huge milestones might disrupt their usual sleeping patterns, preventing them from going through the night.

Also, many toddlers undergo sleep regression upon reaching around eighteen to twenty-four months old because of certain factors like night terrors, nightmares, separation anxiety, teething, and fear of the dark.

Apart from familiarizing yourself with the specific ages or stages when sleep regression usually occurs, it is also advisable to determine the specific signs that indicate sleep deprivation. This is not just for your toddler, but also for what you as their caregiver may experience. That way, you can immediately take action if anyone shows severe signs of sleep deprivation that should be a cause for concern.

Signs that Your Toddler is Sleep Deprived

So, how do you know if your toddler is already sleep deprived and starting to display symptoms of health issues and other unwanted behaviors? Here are the usual signs you need to watch out for:

- Clinginess and constant tantrums
- The tendency to reject drinks and foods
- Crying more often than usual
- Complete meltdowns in public places, like in grocery stores
- Problems with concentration
- Being hard to wake up in the morning
- Tending to sleep spontaneously during the day or take naps unintentionally
- Irritability and moodiness
- Prone to getting frustrated easily
- Crying and getting angry easily

Certain fluctuations in your toddler's sleeping patterns are natural during their first few years. Remember that just because your toddler sleeps the entire night upon reaching three to six months does not necessarily mean they will continue to do so for the full duration of their growth and development. Eventually, their patterns may be disturbed, causing them to have a hard time reestablishing a normal and regular sleeping and waking cycle.

When Should You Seek Medical Advice?

You should also know that more severe sleep deprivation symptoms of in toddlers might require a faster and more proactive response, like visiting your doctor. While it is true that your toddler's inadequate sleep brought on by sleep regression tends to go away naturally after a while, it is still advisable to contact your doctor if they display more alarming symptoms.

Do not also hesitate to visit a doctor if you have any questions about your baby's sleep or want to discuss identified causes of their sleep problems, such as persistent nightmares. Aside from those, the following warrants a doctor's visit or consultation:

• **When your toddler has breathing difficulties** – They may produce noise when breathing, stop breathing for a while when asleep, or snore. Those signs usually indicate sleep apnea. One thing to take note of is that babies below six months often experience irregular breathing.

They also most likely pause in between breaths for around five to ten seconds. However, if your toddler tends to breathe or snore loudly, wake up choking and gagging, or pause their breath for at least twenty seconds, do not hesitate to seek your doctor's advice as it might be sleep apnea, which requires immediate treatment.

• **When you notice that your toddler displays unusual nighttime behaviors** – These include having an unexpectedly high number of nighttime awakenings or fears that only become apparent at night. You also need your toddler's pediatrician's or doctor's advice if their sleep problems start to affect their daytime behaviors.

• **When they display signs of gastroesophageal reflux** – One of these signs is frequent spitting or vomiting of substantial amounts of consumed milk. They may also tend to wake up screaming due to pain. This condition usually occurs when the valve connecting the esophagus and stomach does not function properly.

When the valve malfunctions, it can force the acidic contents of your toddler's stomach back up into their esophagus and mouth. It can be a serious condition that requires medical treatment, so be observant of your toddler's symptoms.

- **When they cannot seem to sleep because of an illness** - If their inability to sleep is caused by pain or fever due to an underlying illness or condition, like an ear infection, teething, or upset stomach, contacting your doctor may be the most viable option for you and will certainly help you to feel more confident.

Just make sure you are also fully knowledgeable of the illness's specific signs or symptoms that warrant a call to your pediatrician. The more serious signs are a fever over 101.5 degrees Fahrenheit (if the child is at least six months old), an earache, swollen glands, and bloody nasal discharge.

You may also consider visiting your baby's pediatrician if you have already applied a specific sleep training technique for over two weeks without seeing any improvements in their sleep. If you do this consistently only to notice your baby is still disturbed during sleep without any apparent reason, their doctor or pediatrician might be able to provide insight or advice on improving the child's sleep.

Also, remember that while true sleep regression and deprivation is not the most fun part of parenting and there is a chance that certain signs and symptoms may require a doctor's help, it is still normal in the majority of cases. If your toddler does not show signs of a major illness that cause them to be unable to sleep, do not worry too much. This stage will most likely pass. Just give it enough time.

Moreover, do not forget to continue sticking to normal sleep and bedtime routines. Make sure these routines are reassuring for your little one. Soon enough, they will get used to sleeping soundly again.

Chapter 2: Understanding Toddler Sleep

A vital aspect of your child's development is sufficient and proper sleep, so you have to make sure that you understand it completely. One thing you have to take note of in this area is that while infants tend to have plenty of sleep, toddlers usually display this strange ability to resist it, especially during times when they need it.

As a parent, it should be your goal to crack the sleep deprivation code of your toddler. That way, you can help them achieve their much-needed restorative rest. If you do not change their unwanted sleeping habits, they are at risk of depriving themselves of the specific amount of rest and sleep they need.

This could lead to them developing behavioral and learning problems, depression, and emotional instability. Inadequate sleep may also make them prone to becoming obese or suffering from other health issues.

How Much Sleep Does Your Baby/Toddler/Child Need?

The first thing you should crack is the specific number of hours of sleep your baby or toddler needs every day, and that will depend on their age. Here is a rough estimate of their sleeping requirements, as well as information about the sleep patterns and habits of babies and toddlers during certain stages.

0 - 3 Months (Newborns)

Newborns, including babies around zero to three months, usually sleep around the clock. In most cases, they sleep for around ten to eighteen hours daily, though their schedules are often irregular. They will likely be awake for around one to three hours daily.

The sleep-wake cycle of infants or newborns also usually depends on their need for feeding, nurturing, and changing clothes or diapers. One vital point to note is that the total hours of sleep required by newborns do not need to be continuous. This means that the period of their sleep can last for several minutes to hours.

Even when asleep, expect the baby to be still active. They may twitch their legs and arms, suck, smile, or generally look restless. If you have a newborn, note that they can show their need for sleep in various ways. Among the signs indicating this is fussing, crying incessantly, and constant rubbing of the eyes.

It would be best for you to put your newborn to bed every time they feel sleepy, instead of when they are already asleep. This move will increase their likelihood of sleeping quickly and training themselves to sleep. You can also encourage your baby to have less sleep during the daytime by keeping them exposed to noise and light and increasing playtime.

You should then turn their environment into a dimmer and quieter one and lessen their activity during the evening. That way, you encourage them to sleep more at night. You are reinforcing the sleeping/waking cycle by doing this.

4 - 11 Months (Infants)

During this age, infants need around nine to twelve hours of sleep at night and around half an hour to two hours of naps during the day, which can be spread out over one to four times. Also, take note that when your baby reaches six months, it is unnecessary to give them nighttime feedings.

This is because they can already sleep through the night. However, only around 70 to 80 percent of babies or infants can master the habit of sleeping through the night once they hit nine months. You may want to start training yourself to put your infant to bed when they are still drowsy rather than fully asleep.

This technique will turn them into a self-soother, allowing them to sleep independently during bedtime and go back to sleep on their own whenever they wake up at night. As much as possible, do not allow them to get used to the habit of looking for parental assistance every time they go to bed.

Infants accustomed to using this behavior are prone to becoming signalers and crying incessantly at night as they need their parents' help every time their sleep is disrupted. Moreover, remember that your infant's developmental and social issues can influence their sleep during this stage.

You will notice that secure infants attached to their caregivers display only minimal sleep issues, but these same infants may also hesitate to give up such kinds of attachment for sleep. Because of that, expect them to deal with separation anxiety that might disrupt their sleep patterns, mostly in the second half of their first year. Other possible disruptions during this stage are increased motor development and any illness.

1 - 2 Years (Toddlers)

If your little one has already reached toddlerhood, the number of hours of sleep they need daily is around eleven to fourteen hours. At around eighteen months, their naptimes' frequency will most likely go down to just once daily, lasting for around one to three hours. You should avoid scheduling their naps close to their bedtime schedule, though, as doing so may only prevent them from sleeping on time at night.

Also, toddlers are at the age when they are more prone to showing plenty of sleep issues, like extreme resistance to going to bed and frequent nighttime awakenings. It is also common for them to have nightmares and nighttime fears. Several factors can cause such problems.

Among them is the strong drive to become more independent and increase social, cognitive, and motor skills. All these tend to interfere with their normal sleeping patterns.

Aside from that, factors like separation anxiety, desire to have independence, and development of their imagination can also trigger sleep issues. To determine if your toddler is already experiencing such problems, watch to see if they start displaying behavioral problems and daytime sleepiness.

3 - 5 Years (Preschoolers)

Preschoolers, around three to five years old, need eleven to thirteen hours of sleep every night. They also usually have short naps, around thirty minutes to an hour or two. Just like toddlers, a preschooler may also have a hard time falling asleep at night. They may also find it difficult to wake up in the morning.

The fact that their imagination is already further developed may also cause them to have nightmares and nighttime fears. The preschool stage is also when sleep terrors and sleepwalking are often at their peak.

6 - 13 Years (School-Aged Children)

When your child becomes school age, around six to thirteen years old, the number of hours they need to sleep daily will be reduced to nine to eleven hours. It is also when more and more distractions can affect their sleep. Among them are certain TV shows and the Internet, media, and computers. These things might cause not only sleeping difficulties but also nightmares.

Besides that, watching TV shows close to their bedtime schedule may also lead to sleep resistance, fewer sleeping hours, and anxiety during bedtime. Moreover, there are things that your child may need to prioritize once they reach the school-age years. These include school and social activities, sports, and other recreational activities that take up a huge chunk of their time. Such demands may also affect their sleep.

Stages of Sleep

Just like adults, toddlers and children also have different stages of sleep. You have to learn about these stages if you want to deal with any sleep-related difficulties your child may be experiencing. Before learning about such stages, though, it is important to remind yourself that sleep is vital, as it is the brain's main activity during your child's early development.

The sleep-wake cycle, or what is referred to as the circadian rhythm, occurs with the darkness and the light regulating it. It also takes time for this rhythm to develop completely, which is why newborns do not have a regular sleep schedule. You can expect such rhythms to start developing at around six weeks.

Upon reaching three to six months, babies will start displaying a more regular sleep and wake cycle. At two, many toddlers have already spent a higher number of hours asleep than awake. This is necessary as sleep is vital for their physical and mental development.

However, as mentioned earlier, certain factors in your child's development might be hampering their ability to sleep and follow normal circadian rhythms. One way to handle this is to be aware of the specific things that happen in your child's sleep—particularly the stages of sleep.

- **Stage 1** – Often characterized by drowsiness, the first stage of sleep is what your baby goes through. Here, they begin to fall asleep, but not deeply.
- **Stage 2** – This stage, also called active or REM (rapid eye movement) sleep, is characterized by your little one twitching or jerking their arms or legs. You may also notice their eyes moving beneath their closed eyelids. It is considered the active stage since your baby tends to participate in the whole process. Their brain is still active, which is also the reason why dreaming happens during this stage.

This stage may also be a time when your baby's breathing becomes irregular. It even tends to stop for around five to ten seconds, which may be due to a condition referred to as infancy's normal periodic breathing. Note that these pauses will not cause the color of your baby's skin to change. After the pause, expect rapid breathing to recommence.

It usually comes at 50 to 60 breaths per minute for around ten to fifteen seconds. After that, their regular breathing pattern returns until the whole cycle is repeated. Most babies usually outgrow this periodic breathing cycle upon reaching six months or so.

- **Stage 3** – After the active or REM sleep, the third stage comes, characterized by light sleep. Here, you will notice your baby displaying more regular breathing patterns and rates. Their sleep will also be less active.

- **Stage 4** - The deep non-REM sleep is the next stage in your baby's sleeping cycle. It is also called quiet sleep. Here, your child is in a much deeper sleep, so expect active movements like twitching to stop. You will notice your baby falling into a progressively deeper sleep. Once they are at this stage, it will be harder to wake them up.

It is crucial to reach this stage, as it is the most vital aspect of sleep. It is the time when your child's body performs its most important functions. This depth of sleep that your child experiences causes: an increased supply of blood to their muscles, significant restoration of their energy, and the stimulation of tissue growth and repair.

This is when their body releases vital hormones necessary for proper healthy growth and development.

In most cases, babies tend to dedicate half of their time to every stage or state. The sleep cycle also tends to be completed in around 50 minutes. Upon reaching six months, thirty percent of your baby's sleep consists of the REM stage. During their preschool age, expect the entire sleep cycle to take place every 90 minutes.

You also have to realize that the sleep cycle does not necessarily progress using the mentioned stages in sequence. You can expect sleep to start at the first stage and progress to the second and third stages. After the third stage, though, there is a great possibility for your child to go back to the second stage before they get to REM sleep.

Once the REM sleep is completed, the body will return to the second stage. It is possible for your child's sleep to cycle through the four stages around four to five times the entire night. Another thing to note is that while many people think of sleep as a passive and inactive process, it has been discovered that the human brain remains active during its various stages.

It is the reason why the body still functions, even when one is asleep. With that, sleep contributes much toward performing a wide range of processes, including cleansing the brain and consolidating memories.

Factors that Disrupt a Toddler's Sleep

This book has lightly touched on the possible disruptions to a toddler's or child's sleep when it comes to the required number of hours of sleep based on age. To understand these disruptions even better and act on them appropriately, they are categorized as follows:

Sleep Changes/Shifts

At around three to six months, many babies may need to make many adjustments to their sleeping patterns. This change or shift in sleep is usually characterized by the need to be awake more during the daytime and sleep longer at night. It is also when the toddler's sleeping cycle begins to resemble that of an adult—alternating between light and deep sleep.

The problem is that if your toddler gets into this stage, they are at risk of being unable to handle the change, causing disruptions to their normal cycle. It may happen whenever they shift between each stage of sleep. This shift may cause them to wake up and be unable to put themselves back to sleep.

Note that this scenario also occurs in older kids and adults. They also tend to wake up at night for such reasons; however, they already know how to put themselves back to sleep right away. Since toddlers and children have not yet mastered this skill, they may lose precious hours of sleep.

Certain Breakthroughs or Milestones

Sleep disruptions in toddlers also often come in the form of breakthroughs and milestones. Note that a lot of parents frequently report sleep deprivation and regression in kids upon learning new skills, like crawling, rolling over, and standing. In this case, your toddler may be overwhelmed with the new skill they have learned.

It might occupy their mind too much, increasing their desire to practice and hone the skill always, even during bedtime. Moreover, if they have just acquired the skill of standing up on their own, there is a great possibility that they will do it all the time in their crib. Your toddler may stand up when they wake up in the middle of the night and may struggle to go back to sleep because they cannot put themselves back down.

Environmental Changes

Another category that may interrupt your toddler's sleep is a change of environment. Note that even minor changes in surroundings can have a major impact on their sleep. Even if they slept well in the past, a sudden change in the weather, for instance, can significantly affect room temperature.

It might lead to discomfort at night, making them unable to sleep. Another possible reason is the new outdoor lighting that penetrates their room. If this is still new to them, it might keep them up.

Separation Anxiety

Your toddler's sleep may also be interrupted by separation anxiety. At six to twelve months, a baby may start to understand whenever they are away from you. If neither parent is in their room, it may cause them to get anxious. The peak of this problem often happens at ten to eighteen months, though it fades once they hit two.

However, you will notice your toddler waking up more than usual at night because of this separation anxiety. They may end up crying, looking for you, or trying to get out of their crib. Your toddler may also have a strong urge to sleep beside you. While separation anxiety is very challenging, remember that it is normal. It is a part of their emotional development, so you should not worry too much about it.

Sudden Changes in Routines

If you suddenly change routines, this may negatively affect your child's normal sleeping patterns. It could occur when traveling together, causing them to stay up late, which they are not used to. It could also occur when they suddenly fall ill, causing them to get used to either parent checking up on them every night.

They may get used to the feeling of being soothed or rocked to sleep because of the illness, so they may want you to do the same even after they have recovered. Note that every time regular routines change, their sleep patterns may be temporarily thrown out of balance.

Possible Effects of Lack of Sleep in Toddlers and Children

Aside from learning about the stages of sleep and the number of hours that your child needs for sleep depending on their age, it is also crucial to gather as much information as possible about the effects of lack of sleep in toddlers and children. That way, you will have an idea of what actually happens if your child lacks sleep or does not sleep the whole night.

By learning these possible effects, you will be more motivated to find ways to correct their sleeping patterns and train them to be a good sleeper.

Poor Cognitive Abilities

If you do not do something to correct your child's sleeping problems, they will most likely be deprived of much-needed sleep, which is essential to boost their cognitive abilities. Keep in mind that sleep is the main nutrition needed by the brain. It plays a major role in the growth and development of their cognitive function.

Adequate sleep is also vital for your baby's body to accomplish its intended functions, especially during the first few months and years of life. Those who sleep well have a better chance of establishing stronger brain architecture than those who do not. The problem is that those who suffer from insufficient sleep may also lose their chance to develop vital cognitive skills as they grow.

Moreover, sleep contributes a lot to raising smart kids. Parents must train their kids to sleep without any interruptions if they want them to grow into faster and better learners. It is because of the importance of sleep in their cognitive function.

With well-developed cognitive skills, your toddler can also display better language skills, focus, and attention spans. With that, expect them to digest and absorb new information with ease. Aside from that, adequate sleep is also vital for creativity. If they do not get enough sleep, their cognitive function will most likely suffer, leading to lower rates of learning and cognitive development.

Delayed Growth

It is also highly likely that your child's growth and development will suffer from a lack of sleep. Sufficient sleep plays a major role in ensuring that they grow properly and at the right pace. Also, toddlers and kids tend to grow daily when they are sleeping properly.

It is the time when the brain releases growth hormones into the bloodstream. If they are deprived of sleep, it might limit the production and release of such growth hormones, leading to a significant delay in your toddler's growth and development.

Prone to Obesity

If your child does not sleep well at night, their body's metabolic development may also be drastically affected, making them prone to becoming overweight. Most toddlers and kids deprived of the right amount of sleep tend to gain excess weight, though at a slower pace.

It can lead to an energy imbalance that can further increase their risk of becoming overweight.

Also, take note that sufficient sleep is needed to maintain a healthy hormonal balance. If your toddler does not get sufficient sleep, it might lead to a hormonal imbalance that further triggers constant hunger. Left uncontrolled, they will be at risk of becoming obese.

Aside from that, poor and insufficient sleep can also be linked to increased insulin secretion. Insulin plays a vital role in the control and regulation of glucose processing. It also contributes to promoting the storage of fats. If your child's insulin level gets too high, they will most likely gain weight unnecessarily. It might even make them prone to having to deal with diabetes. Therefore, having too little sleep can raise your child's insulin levels, thereby boosting their chances of becoming overweight.

Poor Memory

If your child has insufficient sleep, it is also possible that they may suffer from a poor ability to retain memories and information. As a result, they may have learning difficulties. Note that the brain plays a vital function of collecting and storing memories created throughout the entire day into a part of the brain that deals with memory retention and habits. It does so to organize such memories, making it possible to retrieve them in the future.

The human brain does such a vital function during the REM stage. It usually happens when toddlers and kids dream. If your toddler does not get the amount of sleep they need every day, there is a high chance that this vital function will be blocked. It can harm their immediate memory.

Other Potential Effects

A toddler is also at risk of displaying the following effects if their poor sleeping habits, including insufficient sleep, are not corrected right away:

- Weakened immune system
- A sudden increase in appetite
- Defiant behaviors
- Overly emotional behaviors: It could be having no patience or very little patience, extreme sensitivity, easily hurt feelings, and explosive temper tantrums
- Medical conditions that may appear in the future

Again, it is worth reiterating that sleep regressions are normal, but if you notice that your child already displays major side effects from their inability to meet their required sleep, taking action is essential. This is even more important if their sleep regression goes over the expected level at this age, around two to six weeks.

You have to start training them to sleep well. You can begin with the sleep training methods that are discussed in the remaining chapters of this book. Before applying any technique or method, though, consider consulting a doctor or pediatrician so that you can better decide what method works appropriately for your toddler.

Chapter 3: Sleep Associations

The first technique a parent can use to teach toddlers and children to sleep well is sleep associations. If you are unfamiliar with it, note that it refers to anything your child or toddler associates with sleep and falling asleep. Common examples of sleep associations in toddlers are their favorite stuffed animals, a blanket, or a pacifier.

Sleep associations encompass not only objects but actions, too—ones that you or their caregiver often do to make them fall asleep. These include nursing and rocking them to sleep or co-sleeping—letting them sleep next to you or their caregiver. Note that kids begin to create these associations early in life.

For instance, if you make your toddler sleep by feeding them with a bottle of milk or rocking them to sleep, they will look for this same routine every time it is bedtime. It would be like reinforcing to them that they cannot sleep if you do not feed them. This habit is good during their first few months, but you need to break this sleep association as they get older as it can be unhealthy. It might promote cavities or become a source of unnecessary and extra calories.

With that in mind, it is safe to say that while there are positive associations, there are also negative effects on a toddler. It is the reason why training your toddler to settle and sleep on their own requires addressing negative sleep associations that they are already used to. It is advisable to get rid of the negative associations and introduce positive ones. That way, your toddler can master the art of soothing themselves without looking for that unnecessary action they have to become familiar with.

Negative Sleep Associations

Negative sleep associations refer to those things that your toddler cannot recreate on their own. This means that if they completely depend on it to get to sleep, they will most likely need your help all the time to find it in case they wake up in the middle of the night.

While these negative sleep associations are fine during your baby's first few months, you must start sleep training as soon as they hit around four to six months by slowly eliminating these things. If you do not, those will also haunt you in the long run as those are the major causes of night-waking and their inability to sleep again without help.

By not correcting this habit, they will most likely continue with this night-waking pattern, negatively affecting both the parent and caregiver and the toddler themselves. Here are just a few of the most common negative sleep associations you should slowly break off if you want to train your toddler to sleep well with no disruptions or interruptions:

• **Pacifier** – Several newborns depend on a pacifier to comfort them. The problem is that sometimes parents take too long to wean their toddlers off using pacifiers. Eventually, the pacifier will turn into a sleep crutch for toddlers and children.

If you let your toddler sleep while sucking on their pacifier and letting it fall out naturally once they fall into a deep sleep, they will look for it whenever they wake up, making it hard for them to go back to sleep. You cannot expect them to sleep again comfortably without it.

- **Rocking to sleep** – If your toddler is used to falling asleep only when you rock them, they will always need you to do it for them whenever they wake. Your toddler will constantly look for you. If you do not break this habit, they will always need your help to sleep.
- **Feeding** – Some toddlers strongly associate feeding with sleeping. It has already been tackled earlier that feeding your child to sleep is not always a good idea, especially long term. You must wean them off this habit as they grow older; otherwise, they will end up always looking for a bottle of milk whenever they wake up, so they can put themselves back to sleep, even if it is unnecessary.
- **Motion Sleep** – This sleep association usually results from putting your baby in the carrier, car, or stroller to make them fall asleep during their first few months. Doing this is not that bad if your baby is still under four months. At such an age, letting them sleep through motion will not have a negative impact, but it will no longer be restorative if you still do it when your baby is over four months. It might even cause their sleep debt to pile up.
- **Co-sleeping** – If your toddler cannot seem to sleep without you in the room, it will eventually cause problems. Besides affecting your toddler's sleep, the need to be around for them to fall asleep will also prevent you from having your much-needed rest.

Note that any sleep association that adversely impacts your toddler's sleep, your sleep, their caregiver's sleep, and other family members' sleep can be considered negative.

If you do not get rid of these things soon, those same things that helped your child sleep in the past will stop them from doing so through the night in the future. Because they have not yet mastered the art of settling themselves to sleep, the problem is that they will then stay awake unless you help them.

How to Correct and Fix Negative Sleep Associations

Once you have identified the specific negative sleep associations preventing your child and yourself or their caregiver from getting much-needed sleep, you must find ways to break these habits. While fixing these issues might be challenging, you can still handle them by applying the right tips. By resolving their negative sleep associations, you and your child will be able to enjoy complete rest.

Just make sure that before starting the fix, everyone at home, including caregivers, is aware of what will happen. Inform them about the need to improve your toddler's sleeping habits. By doing that, no one will give in whenever your toddler looks for the items they need to get to sleep.

Also, make sure you are firm in changing the perception of who is fully in control at home. Do not make the mistake of giving in to your child's persistent misbehaviors and tantrums, as it may only ruin their progress during training. True, it is extremely hard to control toddlers' behavior, especially because they still do not understand right and wrong.

As a parent, you should be responsible for setting and maintaining firm boundaries and guidelines regarding sleeping routines and bedtime schedules. You will only set yourself up for failure during sleep training if you give in and let your child do what they want just because of their stubbornness and loud and incessant crying.

To help you even further when it comes to breaking off negative sleep associations, make a point of following these tips:

Create a Plan that You Can Implement Consistently

Create a plan that you can easily follow through on. It should be something that you and your toddler are comfortable with. That way, you can be consistent in implementing it. For instance, you can create a plan that will cultivate the habit of letting your toddler sleep at a specific bedtime.

Set up more positive bedtime routines that will prepare them for bed. Examples are brushing teeth, a warm bath, and dimming the lights. These routines will signal that it is nearly time for them to sleep. As soon as your child can make minor decisions and choices related to sleep, let them do so too.

For instance, you can let them choose what they want to wear to give them more control over the situation. Giving them some control can encourage them to be ready for bed on time.

Determine the Specific Sleep Association You Intend to Break

Identifying the specific negative sleep association that you intend to eliminate from your child's habits should always form part of toddler sleep training. Note that the best time for you to break it off would be when your baby is around six to twelve months, but you must be very specific and learn as much as you can about negative sleep associations.

It is something that can negatively impact your baby's ability to put themselves to sleep. These include a pacifier, which they can insert into their mouth on their own, a comfort blanket, and white noise. Your goal should be to look for those sleep associations categorized as dysfunctional.

Among these dysfunctional sleep associations are co-sleeping with caregiver or parents, a pacifier that your baby cannot insert into their mouth on their own—requiring you to reinsert it several times every night—and feeding them to sleep. Those are the things that you should focus on removing from your child's habits.

Find Out How You Intend to Remove the Sleep Association

You must decide whether to do it gradually or go cold turkey—which means eliminating it completely and immediately. If you go for the gradual approach, you can slowly get rid of the item they often use to sleep. Just set a certain timeframe when it should be completely removed. Find out which approach—between the gradual and immediate—your child will most likely respond to positively.

Reduce Liquid Intake

Try to reduce the amount of milk or liquid your child gets from the bottle if they associate it with falling asleep again whenever they wake up at night. It is also highly recommended to stretch the specific period in between each feeding throughout the night.

You can substitute this reduction in liquid or milk intake by providing them with more calories throughout the day. Avoid expecting too much, though—even if your baby can sleep for longer than eight hours every night, without feeding or nursing, if they are less than four months old and weigh less than sixteen pounds, they still need feedings.

Remove the Sleep Association Every Time

It would also be best for you to train your child to sleep independently without the sleep association, meaning without you in the room or close by. Just promise them that you will see them when they wake up in the morning.

When doing this tip, you can go for either the modified or unmodified approach. The unmodified approach prevents you from seeing them in their room until the morning. Do make sure that their room is completely safe. Remove anything that might put them in danger.

On the other hand, the modified approach involves checking them regularly, yet you have to do it at an increased time interval. You also have to do it without having to reintroduce the negative sleep association they are used to. Be firm and do not give in, even if your child displays tantrums.

Put Them in the Crib when They're Sleepy

Instead of continuing the habit of putting them into their bed or crib only if they are asleep, do it when they're still awake but already sleepy. This is the approach you have to apply if your child's sleep association involves rocking or swaying to sleep. In case they cry, you can come to their room to offer reassurance using touch and words. Avoid picking them up, though. Also, stretch the period before you return to their room whenever they cry. Do it slowly, so they can also gradually familiarize themselves with the routine.

Be a More Effective Communicator

In case you notice your toddler feeling bad or crying when you leave them or their own, give them verbal reassurance that you are still around, but they have to stay in their bed so that they can fall asleep. If they get out of bed, take them back without arguing, talking, or making a tremendous fuss.

Keep in mind that it is the tone of your voice that they will hear instead of your words, in most cases. With that said, do not raise your voice or speak at a fast pace. Maintain your reassuring tone and make sure that you do not show any tension in your posture or face.

This will increase your chance of successfully putting them back to bed and leaving the room without them making an enormous deal out of it. It can make them realize that it is indeed time for them to sleep, and you are serious about sticking to that schedule. Be firm when doing this and make sure you continue to communicate with them effectively.

Introduce Positive Sleep Associations

Remember that sleep associations are not entirely negative. This is because some can produce positive results. You have to do introduce these positive sleep associations to your toddler so that they will take advantage of them instead of the negative ones. Learn about these positive sleep associations in the next section of this chapter.

Positive Sleep Associations Defined and How to Introduce Them

Positive sleep associations are among the most favorable elements that you can use for successful toddler sleep training. As the name suggests, these things are all positive, meaning they can make your toddler feel good about the thought of sleeping. Aside from being favorable for your toddler, these things are also good for you.

These associations are positive and will help to guide your baby to sleep the entire night independently. When they do that, you or their caregiver will also gain much-needed rest. Introducing positive sleep associations is crucial if you are already working on the stage of breaking off negative sleep associations, like having to hold, feed, or rock your child to sleep.

To help introduce positive sleep associations and replace negative ones, you must know examples of them. Among those positive associations that can get your child involved are the following:

- Rubbing, biting, or holding a comfort blanket or lovey
- Singing and humming
- Sucking on their fingers or thumb
- Rocking back and forth on their own
- Banging their feet against their mattress
- Lifting their legs to get them into a fetal position

Make sure that you introduce those that your child can do independently, so they can train themselves to get settled to sleep without your help or the aid of their caregiver. You may also want to introduce positive external sleep associations.

These refer to those things capable of setting the scene or environment for sleep. They also refer to all those positive cues telling the child it is already bedtime. The external sleep associations your toddler can use are:

- White noise
- Blackout shades
- A room temperature between 68 to 72 degrees
- A lovey designed to comfort toddlers and kids and make them soothe themselves

It is advisable to slowly introduce positive sleep associations while also starting to break off the negative ones. For instance, you may want to introduce a sleeping bag to comfort the child if they are used to getting fed for them to fall asleep. Feed them to sleep while you zip them into their sleeping bag.

Tuck a small blanket between you and them while you are feeding them from a bottle. This can make them associate the blanket and the sleeping bag with you and the cozy feeling brought on by it with sleep. Eventually, you can put them down while they are still drowsy and not fully asleep.

Also, soon enough, you can finally put them to bed awake and fully settled while they cuddle with this blanket and snuggle on their sleeping bag. You can do this slowly until you no longer need to be around to make them fall asleep.

You can find other healthy and positive sleep associations and habits you can introduce to your child. Just make sure you pick those that are suitable for them and your family's needs and meet the recommendations of a pediatrician.

Another way to develop positive sleep associations is to build out-of-the-nursery sleeping and bedtime routines. This means you can still rock, cuddle, and feed your child but out of the nursery or their room. You also have to do all these things when your toddler is still awake. By doing that, they will not associate sleeping with them having to sit with you or their caregiver in the rocker before you finally put them in their crib.

Moreover, one thing you have to remember about introducing positive sleep associations is that they are intended to help your toddler learn the basics of self-soothing. That way, they can naturally create positive sleep associations and use them whenever they wake up at night. This means you no longer have to get involved in putting them back to sleep.

Just make sure that you completely get rid of negative sleep associations so they can create new and positive ones on their own. Another thing to remember with using this technique to train your baby to sleep is to practice consistency. You must be consistent while training them, so they can finally sleep the entire night independently.

Chapter 4: Night Feeding

One of the sleep associations discussed earlier is feeding your baby to sleep at bedtime. However, take note that some babies and toddlers also get used to the habit of not only feeding at bedtime but also whenever they wake up in the night when they want to experience the same thing because they associate it with going to sleep.

This means they cannot fall asleep again unless you offer them a bottle of milk or your breast. This is called night feeding, which is elaborated on later in this chapter. One key thing to take note of is that night feeding is actually good for babies. It can help them fall asleep or go back to sleep quickly at night, but it will no longer be a good idea once they get older.

Aside from the risk of disrupted sleep affecting both of you, they are also at risk of taking in more calories and feeding more than is necessary. This is because there are times when your baby looks for a bottle or your breast in the middle of the night for comfort rather than hunger.

If you think it is already time for you to wean your toddler off the night feeding, make sure you are truly prepared for it. Arm yourself with information about how you can do it successfully and expect resistance.

When Should You Stop Night Feeding?

Before you wean your child from milk bottles, make sure they are truly ready for it. The following are signs that it is indeed time for you to stop feeding them at night:

• **They are growing well** - Observe your toddler's growth and development. If you notice they are growing well, maybe it is safe for you to stop the night feeding. If you notice their growth is not yet enough, delay the weaning a bit as they will still need the additional calories from night feeding to grow.

• **They are at least six months old** - Another thing you have to consider is the age of your child. Note that infants fed with a bottle can already be weaned off night feeding as soon as they reach six months. If you are breastfeeding, it may take longer. You may even have to wait for at least a year to wean.

• **They tend to wake up inconsistently** - You will also know it is time to wean your child from the night bottles if they tend to wake up at different times during the night. It is a sign their sleep disruptions are not truly brought on by hunger, making night feeding unnecessary. There are also instances when they wake up because they want comfort and help to fall back to sleep.

• **They have less of an appetite during the day** - If you notice your toddler eating less during the daytime, and waking at night to have a feed, maybe it is time to start weaning. It could be that they are asking to be fed at night out of habit.

- **They have dietary changes** – Some babies who have been introduced to solid foods tend to stop feeding at night on their own. If your baby is not one of them, the time when you introduce solid foods to them should also be when you should start gradually weaning them off night bottles. You need to stop night feeding as they already receive additional calories from solid foods.

One thing you should know, though: Even if they display any of the symptoms above, every baby is unique. It means that each night-weaning adventure is also different. If you want to wean them from night feeding, you should remind yourself it is not a good idea to do it during a time when major transitions occur, like when you are switching or moving jobs.

It is not also advisable to make changes to your baby's habit that will significantly affect their sleeping schedule if they are suffering from an illness or dealing with a growth spurt. Moreover, avoid doing the weaning if you will be on a family vacation or during holidays.

Note that no matter how gentle and gradual your chosen night weaning approach is, you still have to do it at the right time—one that will not cause your baby to deal with one stress after another. Try to wait for the right moment. It should be that time when you and your baby are calm, and they seem to be fully prepared for the huge change.

Effective Tips to Stop Night Feeding

If the timing is right and you think your toddler can already handle the weaning, you should be ready to apply those tips that will work for them. Also, constantly remind yourself that you need to listen to the needs of your baby. If a specific tip or technique does not work at first, go onto something else. Do try it again in the future, though.

To make the night weaning more manageable, here are a few tips you can apply:

- **Water down the milk** – This tip is gentle but highly effective in weaning your baby off the bottles at night. What you should do is to dilute their milk slowly using water. Do this for a few nights.

For instance, on the first night, you can offer them a bottle with 75 percent milk and twenty-five percent water. Gradually reduce the percentage of milk over the next few days until each bottle is 100 percent water.

In most cases, offering pure water for a couple of days can make them realize that they do not have to be fed milk to fall asleep. With that, you will notice them starting to resettle themselves and master the habit of sleeping through on their own.

- **Address their hunger clock** – It is one of the first steps you have to undertake when trying to stop your child from feeding at night to make them sleep more peacefully. You can do this tip by ensuring they get most of the calories they need daily during the daytime.

It, therefore, means you have to avoid waiting until nighttime for them to feast. To make this tip work, have a record of everything that forms part of their daily diet. Once you have a log or record of their daily diet, consult your doctor, especially if you are not yet sure about how you can meet your child's daily nutritional needs.

Also, make sure that they are not extremely tired every time you put them to bed at night. By making sure they get proper rest—and enough of it—they will be able to accept certain changes in their diet, as well as correct their hunger clock much easier. You also have to be consistent, so you can successfully integrate the new habits into their system.

- **Go cold turkey** – Many consider this tip as the quickest technique when it comes to weaning babies and toddlers off the bottle. However, be fully prepared if you intend to follow this approach as it requires a strong commitment.

Also, make sure you are tough enough to implement this approach since you will most likely encounter many late-night protests and tears from your toddler. This is because this technique involves the immediate and complete removal of the night feeding.

It might be necessary for you to substitute the milk feeding with other effective strategies for sleep training, like a gradual retreat and controlled cycling. These alternative strategies can help your child develop the important skill of self-soothing, allowing them to go back to sleep without the bottle.

When you plan to go cold turkey, be strongly committed to the entire process. Never give them your breast, a bottle, or a feed. But be observant when implementing this approach. If you notice them become sick all of a sudden, it would be much better to stop doing it for a while and continue when they recover.

- **Gradually reduce the amount of milk they drink at night** – You can expect this tip to work whether you feed your baby using formula milk or breast milk. What you have to do to make this tip work is lessen the volume you offer to your baby or toddler. It could involve less milk in the bottle or decreased time of breastfeeding.

When using this technique, it is also highly recommended to do another sleep training strategy, so your child will immediately get your message that the milk offered is the only drink available. Knowing that, they can also start to practice the art of self-settling whenever they need to return to sleep.

Moreover, make it a point to make a reduction or change gradually. If you are breastfeeding, be ready to deal with a lot more challenges since your baby will most likely have negative responses. They may respond by pulling, grabbing, and protesting whenever you take them off your breast.

With that in mind, never start this tip if you do not have a solid sleep training strategy that will surely work along with the decreased feeding. You should further try to curb your toddler's habit of falling asleep with a bottle or your breast.

- **Nurse more during the day** - Another way to wean your baby from night feeding is to increase the frequency and volume of nursing or bottle-feeding during the daytime. For instance, you may prefer to give them milk every two hours or so instead of the usual three to four hours.

By doing that, they can consume more milk throughout the day, which will most likely lead to a lower chance of asking for milk at night or waking at night just to feed. Also, make sure there are no distractions whenever you feed or nurse them during the day. They will also start to associate drinking as a daytime activity rather than assuming they should do it at night.

Do the nursing or feeding in a room without any distractions. The room should be dim and should have closed doors. If you have other older kids, get them busy, so they will not disturb you and the baby whenever you nurse or feed. Moreover, try to nurse when you are lying down.

Note that babies and toddlers tend to get easily distracted when you feed them during the daytime, causing them to consume less milk than necessary. The problem with that is it might lead to them making up for insufficient milk consumption by feeding more frequently at night. If they do that, you have to be serious about eliminating distractions during daytime feeding so you can maximize it for both them and you.

- **Introduce a cup early** - If possible, introduce your baby to a cup before they turn one or two. Note that it might be harder to stop your child from night feeding as they get older since there is a high chance they will get emotionally attached to your breast or their bottle.

They may associate it with sleep, contributing to the development of the habit of searching for the breast or bottle whenever they wake up if you have decided to use a cup, bottle feed, or nurse at scheduled times. Set a schedule for using the cup too. You may want to use the cup during daytime hours together with solids.

- **Try dream feeding** – This means waking or half-waking them to have an extra feeding at night. The goal here is to make sure their stomach is full enough, so they have a lower chance of waking up and looking for milk in the middle of the night.

You should do this extra feeding before your bedtime, so they will be full enough until both of you are well rested. Another way to do it is to wait for them to wake up and give them a feeding, provided it has been over four hours since the time you last fed them. Do not give them another feeding until they get up in the morning.

One more thing to be aware of is that babies' and toddlers' internal timetables—as far as sleeping through the night is concerned—greatly differ. With that in mind, you can see parents being more comfortable with the thought of allowing their babies or toddlers to lead in terms of night weaning. However, other parents and toddlers tend to deal with a significant decline in the quality of their lives because of night nursing and feeding.

With that said, observe your own situation and your baby. If you notice the night feeding or nursing does not seem to work for both of you, start making changes. Integrate new habits and changes into your usual routines while still considering your child's needs.

You should have the primary goal of maximizing the quality of sleep for everyone. Keep track of your progress so you will know if the night weaning techniques you have implemented work. If such is the case, you can pat yourself on the back for that major achievement. If it does not seem to work, do not give up, as there are still plenty of available strategies. You just have to figure out which one works for you and your baby.

Is it Necessary to Wean your Toddler from Night Feeding?

As a parent, you may have many concerns about stopping your child from feeding at night, especially if they are already used to it. But if you notice it is already affecting their supposed-to-be peaceful sleep and yours, or the sleep of your family, it is necessary to start weaning your child from this habit.

To start training them to resettle without feeding, you have to decide it is indeed necessary for them to let go of the habit. Also, make sure everyone involved in taking care of them commits to trying their best to help them resettle at night by stopping night feeding.

Do not give in to the urge to give them a bottle just to stop them from crying, as it may only lead to confusion. It might also result in you having to spend more time than usual to wean them from the bottle. Your goal is to train them to sleep without the need to rely too much on bottles or feeds.

Another point to remember is that your decision to wean your child ensures they will not get too many unnecessary calories from milk at night. Apart from that, you can expect them to start eating more during the daytime. This is a good thing if you want to train them to eat healthier, solid foods and supply their body with all the nutrition they need by correcting poor eating habits.

The good news is that by deciding to take bottles and feeds away at night, you will notice a quick and significant improvement in the quality of their sleep. Just be consistent and get everyone on board when it comes to implementing the plan, and you will see your toddler quickly adapting to the new habit and sleeping soundly through the night.

Chapter 5: The Co-sleeping Toddler: To Encourage or Prohibit?

Co-sleeping is a popular sleeping arrangement for new parents, especially those who have just gone home with their new bundle of joy. This sleeping arrangement usually involves sleeping in the same area as your baby sleeps. It does not necessarily mean sleeping in the same bed.

As long as you are close to your child and are in the same room, it is already called co-sleeping. It is more on sensory proximity than physical proximity. In other words, you are co-sleeping if you are in one exact spot where you can smell, touch, hear, or see them without any obstacle.

It is a broad concept that covers various sleeping arrangements, including the following:

• *Bed-sharing* – This involves letting your baby sleep with you and/or your partner every day.

- *Sidecar arrangement* – This is the secure attachment of a crib to one side of the bed, usually on the mom's side. All the other sides of the crib stay intact, except for the one next to the parent. This specific side is taken out or lowered so the baby and mother can easily access each other. If you plan to have this sleeping arrangement, take note that you can use a commercial co-sleeper or a sidecar crib, which attaches easily to a bed.

- *Multiple beds but set up in a similar room* – These could include a crib or bassinet set up close to the parents, usually within just an arm's reach. This arrangement may also include a bed or pallet for your older child set up at the foot of your bed or the floor next to your bed.

- *Welcoming your child into your bed whenever necessary* – Using this arrangement, you have already set aside a bedroom for your baby, but you are willing to welcome them into your bedroom anytime. Many families practice this, letting their kids begin their sleeping hours in their separate bedrooms but allowing them to get inside their parents' room when they wake up at night.

While co-sleeping is generally beneficial and practiced in many cultures in different parts of the world, keep in mind that there has also been a mix of opinions about this practice, as it has a few risks. Also, note that while other cultures perceive co-sleeping as a natural solution for letting parents have enough rest while bonding with their babies, a few also focus more on privacy and independence and do not agree with the practice.

Still, many parents are fully aware of the many good things that co-sleeping can offer. It is more beneficial during the first few months of your baby's life. As soon as they get older, it would be best to let them transition to sleeping in their own area or room because co-sleeping may no longer be as beneficial for your child when they get older. If you do not do the transition at the right time, they may end up having problems with their overall quality of sleep.

The Proven Benefits of Co-sleeping

As mentioned earlier, co-sleeping carries several benefits during the early stages of the child's life. It is for this reason that this practice is encouraged in many cultures and families. The following are just a few of the advantages that you and your baby can get from deciding to co-sleep:

Promotes Long and Sound Sleep for You and Your Baby

One major advantage of co-sleeping is that it allows your baby to sleep longer and more soundly. It is mainly because your baby will be more at ease when they feel like you are just next to them. Aside from that, letting them sleep beside you also means that you get to respond to their needs right away. It further gives them a sense of safety and security.

It also promotes better sleep for you, as you no longer need to get up, turn on the lights, and walk to their room whenever they cry or suddenly wake up at night. Whatever is causing them to wake up, you can address it at once. With that, both of you can return to sleep easily and without too much fuss.

Promotes Successful Breastfeeding

By putting your baby close to you, you have a higher chance of becoming successful as a breastfeeding mom. Many moms agree that the key solution for successful breastfeeding at night is co-sleeping. Co-sleeping and breastfeeding even go hand-in-hand since babies who sleep together with their moms tend to breastfeed more often than those who sleep independently or separately.

It will also be less stressful for you since you do not need to get up anytime at night and visit their room to nurse. The only thing that you must do if you are co-sleeping is to help them latch properly, so both of you can go back to sleep. Through co-sleeping, you can nurse without having to wake up completely. Thus, it will be much easier for you to enjoy a complete sleep cycle and get enough rest.

Moreover, your position when sleeping together with your baby seems much safer for them than when you surround them with smothering pillows and harmful blankets. Just make sure that you create a nightly routine that you and your baby can follow so both can enjoy a restful and uninterrupted sleep.

Offers a Great Bonding Experience

Co-sleeping also seems to work well for a lot of parents, particularly those who cannot seem to give their entire time during the day to their babies because of work and other personal matters. If you are a working mom, you are at risk of not spending a huge part of your time caring for your baby.

In that case, the only period when you can bond and spend quality time with them is at night, which is why co-sleeping is much better for you. If you put them in another room, you will be deprived of the chance to enjoy precious bonding moments with them. Co-sleeping is a much better arrangement if that is the case, as it will strengthen and reinforce your closeness.

You can cuddle and do things that they will surely love, like singing them to sleep or reading a bedtime story. Those are just minor rituals and activities, but they are often enough to promote an excellent bonding experience and make your baby feel safe and secure with your touch.

Increases Your Awareness

Co-sleeping also promotes better awareness about all their movements, and you will be more aware of their movements subconsciously. Such awareness is a huge advantage that you will instantly notice if your baby shows movements that are no longer normal, such as having a high temperature or experiencing breathing pauses.

You will also become more aware of your baby's needs. For instance, you will know right away if you need to change their diaper or cover them up with a blanket. Moreover, you can immediately respond to anything that makes them uncomfortable before it disrupts their sleep. The fact that they are close to you is also a huge advantage in case of emergencies.

Are there Disadvantages to Co-sleeping?

While co-sleeping presents numerous advantages to both the baby and parents, it is still vital to learn about a few disadvantages. That way, you can better decide if this arrangement is one you should be encouraged to do at home or prohibit. The following are a few of the most common disadvantages when it comes to considering co-sleeping:

- *May prolong breastfeeding at night* – Being close to your baby when sleeping at night makes it much easier for them to access your breast for feeding. It is convenient for both of you but can also cause problems in the long run, especially if it causes the feeding to take longer than usual. With prolonged breastfeeding time at night, delays in the specific time when your baby falls asleep may occur.

- *Potential safety issues* – This is because your baby may be at risk of being suffocated or crushed when you share the bed. Aside from that, this arrangement also tends to increase the risk of SIDS, which stands for sudden infant death syndrome.

SIDS refers to a baby's sudden death because of suffocation. It affects babies below one-year-old due to things like loose sheets and blankets that tend to stop them from breathing. Parents are also considered as risks to their newborns or babies when co-sleeping.

This is because they have the potential to roll over and crush their babies. Moreover, certain habits of parents, such as smoking and drinking, can further raise the risk of SIDS.

• *Can somewhat interfere with your sleep* – If you share a bed with your baby, your sleep may be negatively affected. It could be because having your baby around will make you want to stay alert all the time. This results in you being unable to sleep deeply. Furthermore, sharing the bed or room with your baby may also prevent you from getting intimate with your partner.

• *May become the cause of your baby being completely dependent on you* – Note that sleeping with your baby can negatively affect their development. This is because it might create a strong sense of dependence. If it takes a long time for you to transition them into sleeping on their own, it will be more challenging and harder for the two of you to separate.

This is one of the reasons you should avoid moving them into a separate room or another bed too late in their growing stages, as doing it later than usual can cause them to feel abandoned or rejected. It would be best to transfer them to their own room or sleeping area at around six to eighteen months.

Do's and Don'ts for Safe Co-Sleeping

If you want to make sure that your baby stays safe during co-sleeping, here are a few do's and don'ts to keep in mind:

• Put your baby to sleep on their back. Do not let them sleep on their side or tummy.

• Use an infant or baby swaddle in place of bedding. Make sure that the swaddle is safe for your baby to use. By doing that, you can lower the risk of having your baby's head covered with the blanket unintentionally when they sleep at night.

• Use a firm mattress. It should be moderately hard. Do not use pillows or waterbeds for your baby.

• Ensure there is no space between the bed and the wall to prevent your baby from rolling out and getting trapped.

- Be a responsible parent. This should mean that you have to stop any unsafe and unwanted habits that might put your baby in danger if you co-sleep with them. Never share the bed with your baby if you smoke, take or use sedatives or drugs, or become intoxicated with alcohol.

- Keep track of the room's temperature. This is to prevent overheating.

- Do not let them sleep between you and your spouse/partner. You should position them beside just one parent and away from the bed's edge unless there is a bassinet beside the bed.

- Do not share a room with your baby unless it is completely smoke-free.

- Do not put stuffed animals, soft blankets, and loose pillows close to their face.

Practicing these do's and don'ts will lessen the chance that your baby will experience SIDS.

How Long to Co-sleep?

If you have decided to co-sleep with your baby, you have to set a timeframe for stopping co-sleeping. This is because while it is good for them during the first few months, it can lead to problems over time. It might even affect the quality of their sleep, eventually.

Note that just like when your baby or toddler can wake you up accidentally if you share a room or bed with them, you can also do the same and wake them. Your baby will be at risk of waking up accidentally if you or your partner snore or talk in your sleep.

Your child may also be disturbed by certain movements, like you getting up and going to the bathroom. If you are a breastfeeding mom, you may also disturb their sleep with just the scent of breast milk. It can cause them to wake up too frequently.

With that in mind, you should know exactly when you should stop co-sleeping and train them to sleep independently. As mentioned earlier, it would be ideal to set up a separate space for them to sleep when they are at least six months old.

Some parents say that it would be much safer and more convenient for them to share a room with their babies for up to a year. Remember that situations vary from parent to parent, though, so you have to weigh the unique factors that affect the entire family. This will give you an idea about the length of time you will be co-sleeping.

For instance, it may take longer for you to separate if your child has health issues than when the baby is perfectly healthy. On the other hand, if they are very mobile and a noisy sleeper, it would be much better to train them to sleep in their own space or room sooner than usual.

You may also be more at ease if you put their room next to yours. As a parent, you are fully aware of your own situation. It would also be best for you to trust your instincts in deciding the safest route to take when it comes to co-sleeping.

How to Transition

If you have been co-sleeping with your baby or toddler for quite a while, but you feel it is already time to train them to sleep in another room, you must make sure that the transition is as smooth as possible. Note that if your baby is already used to sharing the bed or room with you, you will find it quite challenging to separate them from you.

To make the transition easier for both of you, here are some effective tips that can help convince your child to sleep in another room and make sure that they can easily adjust to the new environment:

- *Have a casual conversation with your toddler or child about the importance of sleeping on their own* – Before giving them their own room, make sure that you exert an effort to talk with them about what you need to do. Let them know about the benefits of sleeping in their own bed and room.

Does your child talk casually? If you think that your child can already understand what you are talking about, try using positive examples such as other kids they know who can now sleep alone. You must make the talk as positive and encouraging as possible, as this tone can motivate them to do what you are telling them to do.

- *Let your child pick the things they need for self-soothing* – Once you have clearly explained to your toddler what it means to transition to their own bed and room, make sure that you allow them to choose things that will make them more comfortable in their new environment. For instance, allow them to choose a bed as well as bedding.

Give them the freedom to pick the transitional objects designed to help them soothe themselves too. By letting them have the things they are comfortable using, the whole sleep training process will become much easier. It is also a big help in preserving their trust, thereby lowering the risk of them displaying unwanted behaviors, especially during the adjustment period.

- *Do the transition gradually* – This means taking simple and small steps. Note that you do not need to make a huge leap right away since it can also result in your toddler experiencing shock with the sudden change. During the first few days, do not expect them to stay in their bed or room the entire night right away. With that in mind, be willing to do the separation slowly but surely.

For example, during the first night of the transition, sit on their bed after your usual nighttime ritual. Try to stay beside them until they fall asleep. Also, be patient during the first night because even if you are around, there is still a high chance that they will be restless since it is the first time they will be apart from you.

Leave only when they peacefully fall asleep. Once they get used to that, you can still stay with them but move farther away while waiting for them to fall asleep. You can stay at the edge of their bed instead of exactly behind them. If they get used to that again, you can move even further away.

Continue moving further away until the time when they can already fall asleep, even if you are not in the room. The goal here is to take simple and small steps, so they can make the necessary adjustments as you do every change until you get to the final stage, leaving them alone to self-soothe and sleep.

- *Teach your toddler some effective ways to fall asleep alone* - Do not just tell them to stay in bed and sleep. You also have to guide them, so they learn a few techniques that will work for them, as far as letting them fall asleep is concerned. For instance, you can train them to close their eyes while on their bed and focus on having fun and exciting thoughts, like plans for their birthday.

The goal here is to let your child have something fun to think about, so they will be more comfortable sleeping on their own and getting rid of any fears and worries even if you are not beside them.

- *Avoid negative nuances* - You need to make sure that you do not let your child have negative nuances about having their own room. For example, if you are expecting a new baby soon, moving them to another room or bed may cause them to think that the new baby will replace them.

With that in mind, it is best to do the transition in a manner that will not make them feel rejected. One way to do so is to move them to their room around three to six months before or after the new baby comes. That way, the two huge events will not overlap.

- *Find the right approach for your toddler* – Note that different approaches for stopping co-sleeping work, but the one that will be effective for you will be that which suits your family's preferences and the temperament of your baby or toddler.

One approach that may work for you is sitting next to them until they fall asleep because your presence will somewhat reassure them. You may also go for the cold turkey strategy. If you are unsure what approach will work for you, do not hesitate to consult a child development specialist or pediatrician.

With a professional's help, you will surely be guided on finding the proper approach to guarantee success when trying to stop the co-sleeping arrangements.

- *Be consistent* – Once you have chosen a comfortable approach for both you and your baby, make sure to stick with it for a long time. Be consistent when implementing the approach. Note that the entire transition process may take up to three weeks, sometimes longer, but avoid giving up.

Continue implementing your chosen approach, even if your toddler puts up huge protests. Do not give in to the tantrums. Remain firm and consistent without forgetting to reassure them that you will still be there for them, even if they are already in another room.

Provided you take the necessary and correct safety precautions, co-sleeping with your newborn or baby during the early stages of their life is generally safe. Also, deciding to co-sleep or prohibit it at home all depends on you. You are the one who determines what works for you and the entire family since every baby, parent, and circumstance is different.

If you have decided to allow co-sleeping, you must make sure that you are prepared to part with your child as soon as they are ready. Note that it is crucial to teach them independence by letting them settle on their own and sleep.

By successfully transitioning them to the habit of sleeping in their own room, you will be more at ease as you see them significantly improving the quality of their sleep. It is also good for you and everyone who takes care of them because better sleep for your toddler also means that you will finally have the peaceful and deep rest you have been longing for.

Chapter 6: Managing Nighttime Fears

Your toddler's nighttime fears could also be among the major factors affecting the quality of their sleep. These nighttime fears will interrupt the intended deep and peaceful slumber, making it harder to train them to soothe themselves and finally sleep on their own.

Also called sleep or nighttime terrors, these nighttime fears are characterized by episodes of intense fear, flailing, and screaming even while your baby is still asleep. You can see this situation happening together with sleepwalking. Just like sleepwalking, nighttime fears and terrors are among the most undesirable occurrences while your baby or toddler is asleep.

Expect each episode to last from just a few seconds to several minutes, but sometimes episodes will last longer than expected. It is also important to note that night terrors differ from nightmares, though the two seem to be the same. One major difference is that unlike nightmares, you cannot expect toddlers or kids with night terrors to wake up immediately from an episode.

You can see them screaming, kicking, flailing, shouting, sleepwalking, sitting up, and looking terrorized, but they will not wake up completely. You may also have a hard time communicating with a toddler or child who has just experienced an episode of nighttime terror. In most cases, you will find these kids inconsolable.

Another thing to note about night terrors is that while they are usually traumatizing, those who experienced an episode can often sleep normally again right after it. Most of them will not even have any memory about the experience upon waking up in the morning.

However, despite that, this can have a great impact on the quality of your toddler's sleep. Sleep training will become even more challenging because of these nighttime fears and terrors. These episodes are not usually dangerous, just disruptive to sleep patterns.

With that in mind, gather as much information about this scenario as possible, including its causes and potential cures, so you will know exactly how you can still train your toddler to sleep well. You can talk with your pediatrician to ease any anxiety that might have been caused by this nighttime terror.

Inform the doctor if your toddler's nighttime fears frequently cause them to stay up, especially for over thirty minutes. A medical professional is important in this case because it is a big help in ruling out other health problems that might cause the episodes of nighttime fears and terrors.

It is also even more important to seek the help of a doctor in case the night terrors happen more often than usual, causing a significant increase in the level of your toddler's daytime fatigue. It is also important to have a thermometer available to determine whether there has been a change of temperature because sleep terrors are associated with temperature change.

Stages of Sleep and How They Relate to Nighttime Fears

Every time you go to sleep, you will undergo a few stages—four stages, to be exact. The first stage is characterized by light sleep, making it easier for you to wake up anyone in this stage. It is also considered as the early phase of NREM (non-REM sleep). The fact your brain is still active during the first stage is also why waking someone up is easy.

As soon as you reach the second stage, expect your mind to slow down, making it more difficult to wake you up. It can transition you to the third stage, considered the deepest phase of NREM sleep. Upon reaching the third stage, it is impossible to wake you up. The fourth stage, referred to as REM, is a phase through which you can immediately wake up. It is because it's the time when your brain activities are too frequent.

Now the question is: How do all these stages relate to the nighttime fears and terrors your child experiences? The answer is that these episodes usually happen while your toddler transitions from the second to the third stage. Your toddler's nighttime terrors often occur in the third stage, and that is the primary reason you struggle when trying to wake them up.

As the nighttime terrors occur in the third stage—the deepest phase of the entire sleep cycle—it may cause them to struggle to wake up. Moreover, it has been discovered that nighttime fears usually occur because of the fear linked to transitioning from one stage to another.

Causes of Nighttime Fears

Nighttime fears or terrors take place once your toddler gets into the deepest phase of the non-REM sleep. It usually happens between 12:00 a.m. to 2:00 a.m., which indicates how much it affects not only your toddler's sleep but also your sleep and anyone else's who takes care of them. It has several likely causes, including:

• *Excessive tiredness* – Exhausted or tired toddlers are more vulnerable to experiencing night terrors. It is because their exhaustion may trigger more brain activities once they fall asleep.

• *Disruptions on their regular sleeping routines and schedules* – Your toddler or child may also deal with nighttime fears and terrors if the bedtime and sleep schedules they are used to are suddenly changed. If the changes happen for a few days in a row, they will be at risk of experiencing night terrors and confusing events.

• *Genes/heredity* – Another potential cause of nighttime terrors is heredity. It has been discovered that certain tendencies to this problem are likely to be genetic. This means that if any of your family members are dealing with these episodes, it is highly likely your toddler will experience them too.

• *Sleep disorders* – This one is kind of serious and has to be corrected right away. If your child displays symptoms of a sleep disorder, such as restless leg syndrome and sleep apnea, they will also be more prone to having episodes of night terrors.

Apart from the mentioned causes, other factors that might disrupt deep sleep, like anxiety, a full bladder, sudden noise, and excitement, can also trigger an episode or two of night terrors as dealing with illnesses disrupt the sleep patterns.

How to Deal with Nighttime Fears in Toddlers

If your child has nighttime fears and terrors and you are planning to start sleep training them, one of the first few things you have to do is address and counter such fears so that they can sleep peacefully. The good news is that it is not hard to deal with nighttime terrors.

Here are a few simple tips that seem to work in many toddlers and children:

Preventing Night Terrors

If you notice your toddler is experiencing more episodes of night terror than usual, there are a few things you can do to prevent them. For instance, you can break up their sleep. You can do that by noting every detail associated with each episode. For instance, you can record the exact number of minutes between when they fall into a deep sleep and when the night terror happens.

Observe them for a few days and record the time when the night terrors strike. Once you are already familiar with the schedule, wake them up fifteen minutes before you expect an episode of night terror to strike.

Let them stay awake for around five minutes. It would be best to let them move out of the bed during that period. Follow this routine for around one week to find out if it works in stopping the night terrors from happening.

Avoid Touching Them During an Episode

This tip may go against parental instincts because the symptoms of nighttime fears in your child may instantly urge you to go to them and hold them, but stop yourself from doing so as picking them up, rocking them, hugging them tightly, or doing anything to touch and calm them down will only worsen things.

Many parents even report that the episode becomes shorter whenever they let it end on its own rather than touching their kids. In your case, you can try lying next to your toddler or child instead while ensuring you are not touching them. It allows you to comfort them and make them feel safe and secure without having to touch them.

Introduce a Bedtime Routine

Before doing so, determine the specific number of hours of sleep your child needs. Note that how much they need to sleep will depend on their age. For instance, babies around four to twelve months often need twelve to sixteen hours daily, including naps. If you have a toddler around one to two years old, your goal is to let them sleep eleven to fourteen hours daily.

You can lessen the number of nighttime terror episodes by ensuring your toddler gets the right amount of sleep. You can achieve that by introducing a bedtime routine, but you must make them follow it consistently. Make sure you choose a simple routine that anyone can easily do, including their caregiver.

The routine should also be something you can do every night. It could be as simple as brushing their gums or teeth before bedtime so that they can associate it with sleep. You may also read something to them before you tuck them into bed at night. You can generate better results by starting to do the bedtime routine before they rub their eyes, as that shows they are already excessively tired.

Stay Calm During an Episode

Every time an episode of night terror strikes, note that the most practical thing you can do is remain calm. It is also advisable to wait a bit for your child to calm down. Never attempt to interact with them or intervene in the situation unless you are one hundred percent sure they are safe.

Keep in mind that while it can be frightening to witness a night terror, it is still not harmful to the child, so you do not have to be extremely worried. You should also stop yourself from waking them up during an episode. Just let them be.

Let them feel your presence without having to interrupt the entire process. Note that even if you try to wake them up, they will still not recognize you. You are even at risk of experiencing more agitation if you try comforting them.

Talk to Them in the Morning

An episode of nighttime terror is something your child cannot remember once they wake up in the morning. It is still helpful to talk with them about it upon waking up.

The goal is to figure out if they have certain worries that are causing the episodes. Just make sure you do the talk somewhat positively. Avoid discussing it in a frightening way, as it might only cause more anxiety on their part.

Offer Comfort and Security

You can also try offering them something comforting and finding out if such an object reduces the frequency of the nighttime fears. It could be a toy that they find comforting.

The goal is to let them hold something that will make them feel protected and secure every time they sleep at night. That way, they will become less prone to experiencing nighttime terrors.

This comfort-inducing item can also come in the form of a night-light. While working through your child's nighttime fears, switch to using a night-light, which is dimmer than a normal light. It should provide dim light while also having a warm and soft hue.

This type of night-light is a big help for kids with night terrors. Avoid bright and blue lights as these may hinder melatonin production in your toddler's brain, preventing them from getting drowsy during bedtime.

Reduce Stress

Try to find out if something is stressing them out. Remember that stress is one of the major reasons kids experience nighttime fears. If you think that your child is stressed, find out the source. Your goal is to lower their stress levels so that they can sleep peacefully every night with no episodes of nighttime fears and terrors.

Moreover, make sure they get enough rest every time. Avoid making them excessively tired. Avoid enabling them to stay up too late. Otherwise, this overtiredness may make them more prone to experiencing more frequent and longer night terror episodes.

Dress Them in Comfortable Light Clothes for Bedtime

This tip is more on preventing the nighttime fears and terrors from taking place. Let them wear light and comfortable clothes before sleeping. Note that you are just increasing your child's likelihood of experiencing night terrors if you dress them in heavy or thick clothes that could cause overheating. Aside from letting them dress lightly, make sure you also tuck them into bed and under a light blanket, giving them the choice of having a larger cover available should they become cold.

Make the Room Conducive for Sleep

Make sure their bedroom is comfortable enough and conducive to sleep. Remove anything in the room that might disrupt their sleep, such as electronic screens and bothersome noises. Also, make sure the room is completely safe to lower the risk of them getting hurt whenever they have an episode.

You should also remember that nighttime terrors usually happen to kids that are too warm. With that in mind, make sure the temperature in their room is always between around 62.6 to 69.8 degrees Fahrenheit (17 to 21 degrees Celsius). The room temperature should be cool enough that they will remain comfortable throughout their sleep.

When Should You Contact a Doctor?

You have to make sure you visit the child's pediatrician, especially if you think the night terrors are no longer normal. Set up an appointment with the pediatrician to determine if your child is suffering from any problem causing the night terrors. It could be that they have certain health problems, like adenoids, enlarged tonsils, or sleep apnea.

By visiting their doctor, your child can undergo the appropriate tests necessary in ruling out unwanted health problems. For instance, for enlarged tonsils and adenoids, a child can undergo a procedure that will remove those problematic parts that obstruct sleep. Once removed, you can expect them to sleep more soundly every night.

In case your child's night terrors and fears become too frequent, the best thing you can do is record anything related to each episode in a sleep diary. Do this for one or two weeks to monitor all factors connected to the problem.

Among those things that you should record are your child's bedtime schedule, the number of hours they sleep every night, the number of hours they wake up at night, how long each episode lasts, and the specific item they use for comfort or to fall asleep.

Record the number of naps they have every day, as well as potential triggers of the night terrors. The sleep diary will be a big help to you and your child's pediatrician, especially with determining the common triggers of each episode. If the night terrors continue, no matter how much effort you put in to stop them, visiting the pediatrician is the best thing you can do.

Moreover, consulting a doctor is wise if your child suffers from any of the following concerning sleep terrors:

- Significant increase in frequency

- Disrupts not only your baby's sleep but your sleep and that of others
- Results in injury or other safety concerns
- Causes daytime symptoms associated with problems in functioning and excessive sleepiness
- Does not have any sign of stopping; for example, if the sleep terrors continue as your child reaches teenage years

With the help of a pediatrician, you can identify the cause of the problem. They can even recommend a sleep specialist who can help your child experience better sleep quality. If the episodes start to affect your child's daily activities, i.e., their performance in school and relationships with family and friends, their doctor may prescribe low doses of tricyclic antidepressants or benzodiazepines—though this is rare. In most cases, night terrors naturally die down as your toddler gets older.

Remember that the doctor often diagnoses night terrors regarding your child's medical history and the result of a physical exam. If they suspect other health issues, additional tests may be given, including an EEG, a noninvasive test that measures your child's brain waves.

This helps to determine if your child has an ailment that could cause seizures. Another test is a polysomnography, a sleep examination designed to determine if there is a breathing disorder. If your doctor does not find any major health concerns, you do not have to worry too much. It usually means your child's case is normal and that the disorder will eventually go away on its own.

Chapter 7: Nightmares and Bedwetting

Another factor that might be a hindrance to successful toddler sleep training is having nightmares. If your toddler often has terrifying nightmares, expect them to wake up in the middle of the night and have a hard time going back to sleep. Their nightmares may also result in other interferences when it comes to falling back to sleep—one of which is bedwetting. How can you deal with the two things simultaneously? This chapter provides you with plenty of helpful answers.

Nightmares in Toddlers Defined

Everyone, regardless of age, experiences nightmares. The problem is that their effects seem to be worse for toddlers and children. If your toddler has nightmares often, these realistic yet unpleasant and bad dreams may have a huge negative impact on their sleep.

It is characterized as a bad dream because it often involves an imagined threat or danger. This means their nightmare may be all about a scary or dangerous situation. Nightmares even come with disturbing images, figures, and themes. These may come in the form of ghosts, scary animals, bad people, and monsters.

Fear of being injured and a complete loss of control are also among the usual themes when your child has a nightmare. While a nightmare happens now and then for many kids, you can expect it to be a more common occurrence among preschoolers or kids around three to six years.

This is because it is the age when kids' imaginations are highly active. It is also the time when they have already developed normal fears that might cause them to have bad dreams.

What Makes Nightmares Different from Night Terrors?

Nightmares are not the same as night terrors. Night terrors cause a child to experience episodes of extreme panic. The child may be confused, cry out, and move around. Waking the child during a night terror is often difficult, and the child rarely remembers the dream that caused the terror.

Note that nightmares in toddlers differ from nighttime fears that were discussed in the previous chapter. One thing that distinguishes nightmares from nighttime fears is the child's level of awareness. This is because a nightmare is something your toddler can remember. If your toddler is more verbal, there is even a chance for them to talk about it with you.

They can discuss it with you since they can usually recall the entire experience vividly. As for night terrors, you cannot expect toddlers and kids to remember the episode upon waking up. Another thing that makes the two different is the time when they take place. You can expect night terrors to disturb your child's sleep early into their sleep, usually after one to two hours.

It could come in the form of partial awakening, so they look like they have woken up, though not completely. Nightmares, on the other hand, often happen during the later parts of the night. You can expect nightmares to disrupt your toddler's sleep after midnight. Nightmares are also different from night terrors in the sense that the former may cause your child to wake up.

They may even cry incessantly and look for you for reassurance and help to calm down. These nightmares may also cause your toddler to experience difficulties going back to sleep. It should be noted that while all people experience nightmares, this situation could be more problematic for toddlers and kids.

This is because while they can recall what happens to them while they are having a nightmare, they still do not understand how to properly explain the problem. Some may find it extremely challenging to discuss the problem, especially if their language skills are not fully developed.

If you are a parent with a child who often has nightmares, part of their sleep training should involve learning how to deal with such issues at night. You will have an easier time dealing with the problem if you know exactly what is causing the nightmare.

By knowing the actual cause, you can use the most appropriate approach to handle nightmares whenever they happen, and you can ensure they do not stop your child from having a peaceful sleep every night.

Common Causes of Nightmares in Toddlers

Identifying the cause of your child's nightmare should be one of the first few steps you should undertake toward solving this specific problem affecting their sleep. One thing to note when trying to identify the exact cause of toddler nightmares is they are usually created by the specific part of your brain responsible for REM sleep.

Among these parts are those vital to processing emotional experiences and those responsible for memory. The problem with nightmares is that they seem real and vivid, which is why their effects can be extremely distressing to your child. Moreover, remember these are normal during the growth and development stage of any child.

However, certain causes can help you guide your toddler or child in dealing with nightmares more efficiently, making it possible for them to enjoy a good sleep still afterward. Sometimes, your child will have nightmares because of hearing or seeing something upsetting during the day.

Another likely cause is a traumatic experience. It might cause fears, leading them to dream about it at night. Your child's nightmares may also arise from their development. Sometimes it happens as a way for them to cope with certain changes in their life.

It could be because of starting school, living with parents who got remarried or divorced, or a recent move to a new place or neighborhood. Nightmares may also result from psychological and genetic factors. Aside from that, they are common among kids who have depression, intellectual disability, and certain ailments affecting the brain. Other potential causes of toddler nightmare you should be aware of include:

- High fever
- Certain medications during or after treatment
- Stress and conflicts
- Excessive tiredness
- Insufficient sleep
- Irregular sleep routines
- Seizures
- Sleep-disordered breathing, particularly caused by sleep apnea

Sleep apnea is probably the most important to identify among the causes of nightmares in toddlers. That is because those who have sleep apnea will not only have nightmares but also display other symptoms, like teeth grinding, snoring, and bedwetting.

Kids with sleep apnea may also have sweaty and restless sleep and tend to use their mouths when breathing. They display growth, attention, and behavioral problems during the day. If your child is diagnosed with sleep apnea, it could be one of the major causes of their nightmares. It is important to treat it by reversing its symptoms, which usually includes resolving nightmares too.

Dealing with Nightmares in Toddlers

Once you have identified what specifically causes your toddler to have seemingly incessant nightmares, it is time to craft a few solutions that will certainly help you and them to deal with each episode. You have to seriously consider finding ways to make your child handle their nightmares more effectively, especially if those disrupt their sleep.

Meaning that even with their night terrors and nightmares, if you train your toddler to sleep independently, it will become easier. The following are just some of the most effective ways for you and your child to handle their nightmares:

• *Make sure they get enough sleep* – One way to lessen the frequency of your toddler or child's nightmares is to make them sleep the required number of hours for their age. They should get adequate sleep and maintain a regular bedtime routine and schedule. This could be a big help toward cutting down the intensity and frequency of their nightmares.

• *Identify your child's fears* – Find out what your child is afraid of. Talk with them to find the bits and pieces of information that will let you pinpoint their fear, especially if they are still at an age when they cannot clearly relay their message. Ask open-ended questions, so they can let you know the specific things that scare them at bedtime.

Avoid making fun of their fears because even the most trivial and funniest things for you are extremely real for them. Learn more about their fears, as doing so can help you find ways to reassure them.

• *Avoid making them believe the imaginative creatures in their head exist* - Never say things that can cause your child to believe the frightening creatures they imagined are real. This means you should avoid telling them that you will save them from it because doing so may only confirm it indeed exists. Try to make them realize that what they're afraid of is just a figment of their imagination and is not true; otherwise, you won't be able to comfort them.

• *Create fun and happy bedtime routines* - This means you should develop routines before bedtime that can make your child feel happy and at peace. Avoid exposing them to scary TV shows, movies, and music thirty to 60 minutes before their bedtime schedule.

Also, do not read frightening bedtime stories or expose them to anything that might be upsetting. You should be able to calm them down and soothe them before falling asleep, so their experience throughout the night will also be peaceful. A calm mind can contribute to preventing nightmares.

Some of those fun and happy bedtime routines that make your child feel relaxed and eliminate worry are putting on their chosen pair of pajamas, brushing their teeth, letting them play with their favorite stuffed toy, and reading a fun and relaxing story to them. You should also use this time to cuddle before you tuck them into bed. It is a big help toward making them feel secure.

• *Talk about their nightmares* - It is also advisable for you to discuss their nightmares during the daytime. Your goal should be to identify a theme or pattern, especially if the nightmares become too frequent. If you have identified a theme or pattern, maybe something is bothering your child.

Maybe they are dealing with stressors that cause them to have nightmares whenever they sleep. Discuss such stressors and try to work together in lessening or fully eliminating them.

- *Create a cozy bedroom conducive for sleeping* – Your goal here should be to create the most reassuring and safest sleep environment for them. Their bedroom needs to be designed in a way that will make them feel safe. It should let them calm down, recharge, and reinvigorate them for another busy day.

One thing you can do to make their bedroom conducive for sleeping is to add a night-light to provide a sense of security. However, it is crucial to go for a night-light with a warm hue. It should not have any blue light either. Also, set the most comfortable room temperature appropriate for sleeping.

Make sure that no disturbing noises will distract them once you close their door. You may also want to invest in a white noise machine and put it in their room to block external and unwanted sounds, which will allow them to sleep peacefully.

- *Offer reassurance* – This tip is something that you should do whenever your child has nightmares. Remember that nightmares can be frightening and unfamiliar territory for kids. With that in mind, you need to reassure and comfort your toddler or child whenever they have just experienced a nightmare.

Tell them that it is just a bad dream. It is not true and will never hurt them. They may think their dream took place somewhere. In that case, help them to understand that it is all make-believe. Let them know that it did not and will never happen.

Also, make sure that you constantly remind them that you are just in the next room. Reassure them that you will always be there to keep them safe from harm. It can also reassure them if you label what they just went through.

While it is important to make them realize that nightmares are not real, avoid dismissing or belittling their experience. What you can do is share with them that you also had nightmares when you were their age—and sometimes still do.

It can somewhat reassure them that someone understands what they are going through, and they're not the only one dealing with it.

- *Comfort them in their room* - Avoid leaving your child all alone right after they have just woken up from a nightmare. Spend a few minutes with them to comfort them by providing extra cuddles. Providing this comfort can make them feel safe. However, you must make these comforting gestures in their bedroom instead of yours.

Even if they run into your room after a nightmare, make it a point to go back to their room and comfort them in there. This tip is vital for sleep training as it can make them realize that their bedroom is as safe and secure as yours. If you practice keeping them in their bedroom even when they have a nightmare, you can prevent them from developing a nightly habit of sleeping beside you in your room.

- *Divert their imagination* - Right after a nightmare, it would not be surprising for your child to imagine the worst out of the situation. In that case, you can help them by diverting their imagination. Guide them to a scenario that could have given their dream a positive result.

You may also turn the experience into a fun game that will stir their imagination. For instance, if their dream is about a monster chasing them, make them imagine what it would be like to discover that the monster was actually their friend who needs their help. This will surely stir their imagination. It can even remove their fears since they will try to act as the savior in the situation.

- *Let them find ways to overcome nightmares* - Teach them a few ways to get over nightmares creatively. Your goal is to help your child outgrow such bad dreams, so they will not feel so frightened that they can no longer sleep again on their own.

You can make them overcome nightmares by reading exciting and calming stories after each episode. Another tip is to let them draw pictures of the nightmare, tear it apart, and throw it away; doing so can make your child realize that they have full control over their nightmares, so there is nothing to be afraid of.

In most cases, treating nightmares is unnecessary. It is because most of these experiences resolve over time without any intervention. However, if your child's sleep quality is drastically affected, you need to do something about it. You can use the tips mentioned above to help them overcome nightmares and train them gradually to sleep on their own, even after a scary dream.

How to Avoid Bedwetting

Bedwetting is common among toddlers and children who have just experienced a nightmare. Your child may wet their bed as a result of the fear brought on by a bad dream. The goal is to avoid bedwetting because the discomfort from it may make sleep training even more challenging as they will struggle to fall back asleep again.

You can lower the risk of them bedwetting after a nightmare with the help of these simple tips:

- *Reduce fluid intake at night* - There is a lower chance of your toddler or child wetting the bed if you lessen their fluid intake a couple of hours before bedtime. Try to shift their schedule for fluid intake. Give them fluids earlier in the day so that you can lower it at night, especially close to bedtime.

- *Set bathroom schedules* – Make your child develop the habit of urinating on a schedule. For instance, encourage them to go to the bathroom to pee every two hours. You should also let them do so before bedtime.

- *Get rid of anything that might irritate their bladder* – Make sure you do not expose your child to anything that might irritate their bladder at night. This means you have to eliminate anything that contains caffeine, like cocoa and chocolate.

Another alternative tip is to lessen their intake of sweeteners and citrus juices, and anything that contains dyes or unnatural colorings and artificial flavoring. Those things might irritate their bladder, making them more prone to wetting the bed at even a minor trigger.

- *Use pull-ups or diapers at night* – Do this even if they are already wearing the usual underwear during the daytime. If your child objects to wearing diapers again at night, you can put it on once they fall asleep. Another alternative is a pair of disposable training pants. A rubber sheet designed to protect their mattress is also a big help.

One more important tip is to avoid making your child feel bad about bedwetting. Do not punish them as it will only make them feel more frustrated, especially if it only happens because of their nightmares.

Instead of blaming them or making them feel more uncomfortable and guilty, let them know that it happens now and then, and both of you can fix it. Encourage them by telling them that they can prevent bedwetting incidents in the future, even if they happen because of a frightening nightmare.

Chapter 8: Sleepwalking and Sleep Talking

Another challenge that you may encounter when training your toddler to sleep on their own is the tendency to sleepwalk and to talk in their sleep. This is because both sleepwalking and sleep talking disturb your child's slumber. The problem is, if they either sleepwalk or sleep talk and then wake up in the process, they may find it extremely challenging to sleep again.

Though, one thing to observe is that these are normal occurrences. In fact, both happen to about thirty percent of toddlers and kids. With that said, either or both of the two can significantly impact your child's sleep, so it is essential to learn about sleepwalking and sleep talking as much as possible.

It is also crucial to learn what you can do to avoid it. Moreover, it helps to find out if any warning signs suggest needed help from a medical professional. That way, you or their caregiver can take immediate and appropriate action.

What Should You Know About Sleepwalking in Kids?

Sleepwalking—also called somnambulism—involves your child's purposeful walking movements that take place while they are in a sleep-like state. This behavior is categorized as parasomnia, a sleep disorder category that encompasses abnormal behaviors and movements during sleep.

Sleepwalking in toddlers and kids is characterized by them getting up even during their sleep while having no awareness of the action. You can often see this situation affecting kids around four to eight years old, but sometimes toddlers experience it too. Most of those who sleepwalk start doing so one or two hours after they fall into a deep sleep.

Each sleepwalking episode lasts for around five to fifteen minutes. Even though sleepwalking is not usually harmful to children and most outgrow the behavior, you still need to know that it is potentially harmful if you do not address the problem.

For instance, there is a risk of your child getting injured when they sleepwalk. With that in mind, you and their caregiver should work together to protect them from potential injuries. One way to do so is to figure out the specific factors that make your child more prone to sleepwalking.

You must pinpoint the cause of the sleepwalking so you can take the right action. Factors that might lead to sleepwalking are:

- Inadequate sleep
- Extreme fatigue or tiredness
- Irregular sleeping schedules, habits, and routines
- Staying in a new and different sleep environment
- Anxiety
- Fever or other illness

- Medications they are taking, like stimulants, antihistamines, and sedatives

If your family members have a history of sleepwalking, be aware that it might also contribute to your child having episodes of it. Each episode differs, but in most cases, your toddler or child will get out of bed or sit on their bed and then walk around their room. It often happens for less than ten minutes.

There are also instances when the sleepwalking episode will include your child putting on clothes, roaming or walking around the entire house, and opening doors. They may open their eyes even if they are still asleep. Their open eyes are also often accompanied by a glassy-eyed and glazed look.

Do not expect a clear answer if you have plans to ask them about what happened when they wake up in the morning. This is because your child cannot recall the sleepwalking episode once they fully wake up.

Also, be mindful that your toddler or child may display other actions and behaviors linked to the condition other than the most common sign of sleepwalking—which is walking while asleep. Other symptoms your toddler may show if they have the condition are:

- Sitting up while in bed and doing certain movements repeatedly
- Walking around the room or house
- Moving clumsily
- Not answering even if you are talking to them
- Mumbling or talking while asleep
- The tendency to urinate in inappropriate areas
- Doing repetitive or routine behaviors, like closing and opening the doors

Another thing to remember about sleepwalking is that while it is common and happens naturally in kids, sometimes it indicates an underlying condition. Conditions that might be linked to sleepwalking are sleep apnea, migraines, head injuries, restless leg syndrome, and night terrors.

How to Deal with Sleepwalking in Toddlers and Kids

If you think your child's case is normal and does not relate to any other major health concerns but are still worried about their safety during each episode, you have to train yourself to do things that will lessen the sleepwalking tendencies.

Moreover, you have to do something about it if you feel like their sleep is already drastically affected. Note that if you do not take action, even if their case is normal, you can experience major difficulties and challenges during their sleep training.

Here are a few practical pieces of advice for you and your toddler's caregiver that should make the child less prone to sleepwalking and guarantee their safety during each episode:

Implement Safety Measures at Home

Note that your toddler or child's safety will be compromised during every sleepwalking episode as they will most likely roam around the house, not fully aware of what they are doing. When they do that, they're at risk of getting injured. That said, it is advisable to implement safety measures around your house.

Among the safety measures that you and their caregiver should try to do are:

- Keeping the doors and windows closed and locked every night
- Getting rid of breakable and sharp items around the bed

- Getting rid of all tripping hazards, not only in your child's room but also the entire house
- Installing window and door alarms
- Putting locks in places that your child cannot easily reach
- Putting on safety gates in doorways and at the front part of stairs
- Ensuring that keys are out of your child's reach
- Preventing your child from sleeping in a bunk bed
- Turning down the hot water heater's temperature to lower their risk of getting burned

Your main goal should be to create a safe and secure home that is sleepwalker-proof. It also helps to hang a bell on their bedroom door, alerting you or their caregiver whenever the child sleepwalks and gets out of their room.

Set an Early Bedtime

This tip is a huge help if your goal is to prevent your child from sleepwalking in the first place. Keep in mind that one of the major causes of sleepwalking, especially in toddlers and children, is excessive fatigue. It can cause your child not only to sleepwalk but also to experience other sleep problems, like nightmares and night terrors.

You can prevent the fatigue that might trigger their sleepwalking by setting up an earlier bedtime and sticking to it. You may set it up thirty minutes to one hour before their usual schedule. The good thing about this tip is that it also helps to improve excessive sleepiness.

You should also try pairing up their early bedtime with relaxing routines. You can create a regular nap and sleep schedule, both for daytime and nighttime. Other routines that will make them think it is already close to bedtime are brushing their teeth, changing into their favorite sleepwear, and listening to bedtime stories or soothing music.

Never Wake Them Up During a Sleepwalking Episode

If you have a sleepwalker, make sure to avoid waking them up every time they have an episode. It will be best for you to guide them back to bed instead. Keep in mind that even if they are asleep, your child will most likely respond to the sound of your voice. Talk to them gently and calmly while guiding them back to their room or bed.

Practice Scheduled Awakenings

You may also wish to try the scheduled awakening technique if you have already identified the usual schedule when their sleepwalking happens. You can do this technique by waking up your child every night at around thirty minutes before the usual time of the sleepwalking episodes.

Try to do this technique every night for one month, and you will notice a significant reduction in the severity and frequency of the episodes. Make it a point to wake them up completely—one where they can hold a conversation. One issue with this technique, though, is that it can lead to sleep deprivation.

With that in mind, ensure they have enough sleep during the daytime to make up for it. Also, try doing this for only a month or just until you notice the sleepwalking episodes dwindling.

Reduce Liquid Intake Before Bedtime

Liquid is vital for your child's health as it helps them stay hydrated. However, it can also cause trouble, especially if they are prone to sleepwalking. This is because having a full bladder can trigger sleepwalking episodes.

With that in mind, make sure to limit your child's liquid consumption at night. It is also advisable to eliminate any drink that contains caffeine. Moreover, it helps if you let them use the toilet before sleep. With that routine, they will have a lower chance of being disturbed by anything during sleep.

Build a Sleep-Friendly Room

Another important tip to prevent sleepwalking and ensure they get enough undisturbed sleep every night is to make their room as relaxing and sleep-friendly as possible. Your goal is to create a quiet, comfortable, and dim sleep environment. It can make them relax and feel the need to sleep.

Ensure that the bedroom's temperature is low—around 75 degrees Fahrenheit or 24 degrees Celsius is the ideal temperature. It also helps to pair this up with relaxing routines, like deep breathing and a warm bath. That way, your child's mind will be conditioned to sleep peacefully without being disturbed by anything, even a sleepwalking episode.

When to Seek Medical Help

There is a possibility of a connection between sleepwalking and other possible ailments and conditions, so you and your toddler's caregiver must be vigilant in recognizing the behavior displayed by your child. You need to observe the child, especially during their sleepwalking episodes. Consider contacting a doctor if your child's sleepwalking episodes happen more frequently.

You may also need to seek professional medical help if you notice your child has a higher risk of injuring themselves or those around them every time they sleepwalk. Another scenario that warrants a doctor's help is if the sleepwalking episodes do not seem to end and continue as the toddler grows older.

You may also need to consult a doctor if you and your child's caregiver notice the following in your child:

- Sleepwalking episodes that start disturbing the sleep of other people in the household

- Extreme sleepiness during daytime
- Over two sleepwalking episodes every night
- The tendency to gasp for breath or snore loudly along with sleepwalking
- Bedwetting during sleepwalking episodes

Just relay the alarming signs and symptoms your child displays during sleepwalking episodes to your chosen doctor. You can then expect them to recommend a specialist sleep center, a place where your child's sleep history and your sleep pattern will be discussed.

If necessary, your doctor will arrange sleep examinations or studies. These studies' goal is to rule out other conditions and ailments that may be causing the episodes, like restless leg syndrome and sleep apnea. In the sleep study, your child will be asked to sleep in a sleep laboratory for a night.

Here, electrodes will be attached to various parts of your child's body. The main objective is to measure your child's brain waves, breathing, heart rate, leg and eye movements, blood oxygen level, and muscle tension. Your child will also be recorded on the camera while they are sleeping.

This study is often conducted if there is a high chance your child is suffering from a more serious condition. For troublesome cases of sleepwalking, your chosen doctor may also do scheduled awakening, a technique that keeps track of your child's sleep for several nights. It helps them to figure out the specific time when the episode often occurs.

Once the usual schedule of each episode is detected, your child will be roused from their sleep around fifteen minutes before such a schedule. It is a big help in resetting your child's sleep cycle and keeping sleepwalking behaviors, especially the more dangerous ones, under control.

Although rare, there are also times when the doctor will recommend the intake of certain medications—one of which is clonazepam. Clonazepam refers to a benzodiazepine medication used in suppressing one's nervous system. If taking the medication, the child will be less prone to getting up and roaming around while asleep.

Make sure to use this medication only in severe cases, though. Remember: It can produce side effects, so talk about it carefully with a pediatrician. Ask whether its benefits outweigh the risks and side effects, and if the medication is indeed right for your child. However, in the majority of sleepwalking cases, the use of medication is not necessary.

What Do You Need to Know About Sleep Talking?

If your child sleepwalks, there is also a tendency that this episode is accompanied by sleep talking. It often occurs if you notice your toddler or child talking, crying, moaning, or laughing even when asleep. Similar to sleepwalking episodes, your child is unaware that they talk during sleep. They will not also recall it once they wake up.

Sometimes, your child's sleep-talking episodes encompass words and phrases you can discern as well as complete sentences. However, there are cases when they talk complete nonsense. Whenever they talk during sleep, you will notice them sounding like themselves or talking using another voice. The things they are talking about can also be linked to past conversations and memories, or they may not be connected to anything.

It is important to consider that while sleep talking is usually genetic and comes with sleepwalking episodes, excessive fatigue and inadequate sleep can also trigger it. Moreover, your child may sleep talk because of stress, and that is why you should set a consistent and relaxing bedtime routine for them.

Just like the things you can do to lessen sleepwalking episodes, you also need to make sure your child gets enough quality and undisturbed sleep—around eleven to fourteen hours to prevent them from talking during sleep. Furthermore, remember that sleep talking usually accompanies night terrors, nightmares, sleep apnea, fever, and other vivid dreams.

You have to closely observe your child to find out if their case is still mild or could be considered sufficiently serious enough to be associated with an underlying condition. You can consider their condition mild if they sleep talk no more than once a week. On the other hand, if it happens each night for one whole month or more, be warier because it can be considered a more serious and pronounced case.

Talk with their pediatrician or doctor about it, and do not forget to ask the expert what to do to handle the case. It is even more important to have it treated if you find that your child's sleep talking is disturbing other members of your household or disruptive in some other way.

What Can You Do About Sleep Talking?

Dealing with sleep talking episodes in children is quite like the ones used to tackle sleepwalking. Tips you can apply are establishing regular sleeping schedules and routines, setting up scheduled awakenings, and ensuring your child gets enough sleep. You can perform those techniques together with the following to further improve its ability to reduce the frequency and severity of sleep talking:

- *Remove all forms of distraction during bedtime* - This includes gadgets, unnecessary noise, blue light, or anything that might prevent them from falling asleep on time. By removing distractions, your child has a greater chance of getting sufficient quality sleep.

- *Practice good sleeping hygiene* - Sleep hygiene refers to practices designed to improve your child's ability to sleep soundly. Among those you can include in their sleep hygiene are setting a relaxing and comfortable temperature in their bedroom and removing lamps producing bright lights close to their bed.

- *Prevent them from eating spicy, greasy, and fatty foods before bedtime* - Make sure they do not drink carbonated drinks either. These unhealthy foods and drinks can cause indigestion, thereby disturbing their sleep and making them more prone to sleep talking.

- *Make sure their bedroom receives enough sunlight during the day* - It should also have enough darkness at night. With that, your child has a higher chance of retaining a healthy cycle for sleeping and awakening.

- *Encourage them to exercise* - Make sure they have enough physical activities or exercise during the day. Good activities include swimming, cycling, and running—however, at this age, this kind of activity will need to be supervised. You may also want to get them involved in sports. Encouraging activity and exercise can significantly improve their sleep quality, translating to a lower chance of sleepwalking and sleep talking.

Just like sleepwalking, sleep talking is often harmless and a natural occurrence in kids. You can even expect your child to outgrow it soon, but if you notice that their symptoms are severe or their condition seems to persist longer than usual, seek the help of your doctor or a sleep specialist.

You can rely on medical professionals to diagnose your child's underlying conditions and issues and subsequently manage them if necessary. They can also guide you on your toddler's sleep training journey, making it as smooth as possible, and helping you remove issues, such as sleepwalking and sleep talking.

Chapter 9: Setting a Sleep Schedule

Have you finally resolved and addressed the issues affecting your child's sleep, like co-sleeping, sleepwalking, sleep talking, and night feeding? Then it is time to develop a sleep schedule for them. The good thing about putting a sleep schedule in place and sticking to it is that it can give your toddler more stability and confidence.

Besides that, your life as a parent and that of the child's caregiver(s) will become much easier. The ultimate secret to setting up a successful sleep schedule is to combine comfort, fun, and structure.

Once you have eliminated all the other obstacles and issues that affect your child's sleep quality, practice the schedule right away. This helps your toddler familiarize themselves with the new routine.

Once they get used to it, you are also assured that they will be more than willing to make adjustments to the schedule as they get older, so it can fit their specific needs.

When Should You Start Setting Up a Sleep Schedule?

Note that as soon as your baby hits two or three months, you can try sleep training them and setting up a regular sleep schedule as this is the period when their internal clock becomes more predictable. When that happens, you can begin to implement basic schedules that fit newborns.

At around three to six months, you will notice their bedtime, wake-up times, and naptimes falling at similar times daily. You can use this information to anticipate the specific times when they naturally feel sleepy, thereby making it possible for you to put them down when they are already drowsy while still awake.

This is necessary as it can train them and help develop a useful skill—falling asleep independently.

What is the Ideal Sleep Schedule for Toddlers?

The answer to this will depend on the specific amount of sleep your child needs. For instance, toddlers need a total of eleven to fourteen hours daily. It should also include naptimes of around one to two hours every day. Also, keep in mind that while toddlers' sleep schedules vary, most of them tend to sleep better when you tuck them in bed by around 7:30 to 8:00 in the evening.

This is because most kids who sleep before 9:00 in the evening tend to fall asleep quicker. They also have a lower risk of waking up during the night, thereby allowing them to get better rest and sleep for several hours. In that case, you can also anticipate your child to wake up at around 6:00 to 7:00 in the morning.

Some toddlers even rise earlier. If your child is an early riser, waking up before 6:00 in the morning, you can rest assured there are still ways for you to make them hit their snooze button. For instance, you can put their favorite toys near them so that they can reach them easily.

If you do that, they will be less likely to call you right away. You may also want to install room-darkening shades designed to prevent natural light from coming in. It can contribute to your child thinking they still need to sleep more until their scheduled wake-up time.

Effective Tips for Setting Up a Sleep Schedule for Toddlers

One important thing you have to think about when it comes to toddlers is that they are notorious for resisting sleep. It is why you really must look for tips and techniques that will let them follow through on a healthy sleep schedule. Your goal is to establish healthy sleeping habits and make sure they follow them.

One way to achieve that is to have consistent naptimes and bedtimes daily. Aside from letting your toddler get the required number of sleeping hours, you can also expect to have an easier time sleep training them. Moreover, once they have a consistent sleep-wake cycle, your life will also start to become easier again with the predictable patterns and a higher likelihood of you getting enough rest and sleep.

For you to have an easier time setting up a sleep schedule for your toddler or child, it is highly recommended to apply the following tips:

Set a Sleep Schedule Based on Your Toddler's Cues

As often as you can, begin sleep training as early as possible. It does not mean that you should already start setting a sleep schedule when you still have a newborn, as you cannot expect them to follow it yet. With that said, you can start trying to modify their internal clock as early as two months.

Your goal is to create a sleep and eating timetable depending on their personality and snoozing habits. Remember to base your child's sleep schedule on their cues. Find out about the specific signs that clearly indicate when they are sleepy. Observe them and determine the usual things they do whenever they begin to feel tired.

For instance, it might be incessant crying, being fussy, or constant rubbing of the eyes. Those actions indicate they already want to take a nap or sleep at night. Your goal here is to familiarize yourself with your child's behaviors and cues, as those will help you craft the most suitable sleep schedule for them—one they can easily follow through on.

Have a Sleep Log

Another thing you can do to establish a good sleep schedule is to have a sleep log. You have to record everything related to their sleep. Doing that will give you a clear idea of the usual time they sleep, making it possible for you to schedule their bedtime and naptime accordingly.

The sleep log will also let you know about their waking windows and sleeping patterns. With that, you will know how much they can handle being awake and the specific time they need to sleep. Note that every baby or toddler is unique, so you have to create a sleep schedule that suits them well.

Set Up a Wake-Up Time

Your toddler should be able to start their day with a set wake-up schedule. As indicated earlier, some toddlers rise early—around 6:00 to 7:00 in the morning. If you notice they wake up later than that, avoid waking them up earlier. Note that you are still starting to set up the most appropriate routines and schedules, so it helps if you let them decide when they can comfortably wake up.

If they already have a scheduled pattern for waking up, try to stick to it because that is more comfortable for them. It is also advisable to let them spend around fifteen minutes slowly waking up on their own. Let them play for a while in their crib during this time before preparing them for the day. It would be best for you to try waiting until 7:00 in the morning to facilitate the beginning of their day.

Incorporate routines that will clearly let them know it is already daytime. For instance, you may want to spend around half an hour dressing them and brushing their teeth and hair. Other routines you can incorporate here include washing their face and letting them use the toilet.

Schedule Breakfast

You may also want to set up a schedule for their breakfast. Depending on their needs, it may be more appropriate to set the breakfast time before brushing their teeth and getting dressed. It is a more suitable routine if they tend to wake up hungry. In that case, it would be best to feed them first so that they will be more likely to cooperate with you once it is time to bathe, brush their teeth, and get dressed.

Make it a point to prepare a light breakfast for them. It should be something they can easily digest. Moreover, try to shorten the amount of time they spend eating breakfast—as this should take no more than half an hour. This will give them more time to play later in the morning.

Include Morning and Afternoon Naps

Naptimes should form part of your child's daily routine as they provide times when they can reinvigorate themselves. It is important to note that not including naps in their daily schedule may affect their sleep quality in the evening. It may also be harder for you to set up a more consistent sleep schedule without letting them nap consistently.

If they are already up by 7:00 a.m., consider setting their naptime around 9:30 to 10:00 in the morning. It should take at least an hour. However, keep in mind that as they grow older, they may also outgrow their morning nap. Do not force them to nap if you feel like they have already outgrown this routine in the morning.

In that case, you may want to fill up their supposed-to-be morning nap with quiet and relaxing activities. You can let them look at books, listen to audiobooks, or play. Allowing them enough quiet time will recharge them, giving them more energy to do more physical activities later in the day.

Set up an afternoon nap schedule for them too. Schedule it after lunch, preferably during the resting period at around 2:00 in the afternoon. As much as possible, do not expect the nap to last for over two hours. Allowing them to nap too late and too long may affect their ability to sleep on time at night.

Establish Routines for the Late Afternoon

You should also include late afternoon routines in your child's daily schedule if you want them to fall asleep at night more easily. Plan these activities after their afternoon nap. It could be a light snack and outdoor activities. It is highly recommended to let them play outdoors, like walking around the neighborhood or in a playground close to your home or letting them run outside in your yard.

Your goal is to let them move, which is good for their body, while also trying to let their energy dwindle before dinner. If you do that, you will have an easier time smoothly preparing them for dinner and bedtime. The fact that you are already trying to use all their energy through outdoor play will also increase their chance of sleeping on a set schedule.

Create Before Bed Routines

You should also establish routines your toddler can do before bedtime. Remember that the first parts of the sleep training will be challenging since you will have a hard time sticking to a consistent daily schedule. Fortunately, you can lessen such challenges by trying to create routines before bedtime.

All it takes is to ingrain such routines into your child's habits until they become used to doing them and associate them with sleeping. Once you begin the training, make it a point to stick to similar routines before bedtime and the same bedtime each night. As much as possible, let your toddler go to bed at around 8:00 in the evening. This is the perfect bedtime for toddlers to have adequate sleep.

The best way to handle the evening and prepare your child for bedtime is to let them play a bit after dinner. After a short playtime, let them do a relaxing activity. It could be reading a book or watching their favorite TV show. Another routine that they should associate with sleep is a nighttime snack (i.e., a glass of warm milk). You may also want to incorporate time for their warm and relaxing bath.

To further make them more accustomed to their bedtime and stick to it, add more relaxing routines, like reading a bedtime story to them or singing a calming and relaxing song. To make them relax even more, give them a comfort blanket or let their favorite toy lie next to them. With a security item close, like their favorite toy, you can expect them to fall asleep faster.

Mistakes to Avoid When Setting a Sleep Schedule for your Toddler

As a parent, it is normal for you to get confused during the sleep training process. It is especially true if you have a somewhat resistant toddler who is quite difficult to train when sticking to a consistent sleep schedule. To somewhat smooth out the process, here are the mistakes committed by other parents when setting up a sleep schedule for their kids:

- *Changing routines now and then* – Recognize that to make your toddler's sleep training a huge success, you need to be very consistent with the bedtime and naptime routines that you are trying to set in place. With that in mind, you have to avoid changing the routines you have already established from time to time.

Never do something like a trial-and-error when encouraging your kids to stick to bedtime routines. It is because doing so may only confuse your child, making it even harder and more challenging to train them to sleep independently. Once a routine is already established, stick to it, and follow it consistently.

- *Not paying attention to your toddler's cues* – Just like what has been indicated in one of the tips mentioned for setting up a sleep schedule, you need to watch out for your toddler's cues. Try to set routines and a sleep schedule based on such cues.

Never make the mistake of establishing a routine based on what only fits your schedule. If you do that, you will miss out on sleep because they already send sleep cues earlier than you have anticipated based on your presently established routines.

- *Establishing too long bedtime routines* – Decide beforehand the amount of time that you can ideally spend on your child's bedtime routine every night. Make sure that it is not too long, though.

Keep in mind that if the routine you make your child follow every night lasts for more than an hour or two, putting them to sleep will be even harder. It would also be difficult for both of you to stick to the routine regularly.

Try to make your child's bedtime routines as short as possible. Go for those that are just enough to make them calm down and sleep faster.

- *Giving in to your toddler's desire to stay up late* – Make sure you do not commit the mistake other parents make by giving in to their kids' desire to stay up late. It could come in the form of letting your toddler play longer because you feel like you have had insufficient time with them due to your busy work schedule.

The problem with allowing them to stay up late and not stick to their usual bedtime schedule is that it can lead to them dealing with excessive tiredness. This can further result in crankiness and a refusal to sleep on time. They can also see you are flexible, which may cause problems in the future.

With that said, make it a point to stick to the sleep schedule you have already set. Ensure the bedtime is right for both of you so that you will not have problems following through on it.

- *Not removing all the distractions from the bedroom* – If you want to be truly successful in sleep training your toddler, you have to make sure that all distractions in their bedroom are eliminated once you have created a sleep schedule and commit to following it.

Some parents believe a great-looking mobile, quiet music, and nice night-light can greatly contribute to their kids quickly falling asleep. It is not the case all the time, though. Take your cues from your toddler's behavior.

In fact, there are instances when these items become distractions, causing toddlers to stay awake even if it is already long past their bedtime. With that said, try only to implement the sleep schedule and routine you created once their bedroom is already distraction-free.

- *Sending mixed signals and messages about your toddler's sleeping spot* - Another mistake to avoid is making your toddler think their bedroom is not the only place where they can sleep. This means you should not let them climb into your bed several times every week, especially during those instances when they become extra fussy and cranky.

Bear in mind that if you let them think they can still share the bed with you, it might cause problems in the sleep technique you are trying to implement and send a mixed message to your toddler. It might confuse them, disrupting their sleep.

To avoid that from happening, be firm and make them follow specific guidelines on where they should sleep. Make them follow the sleep schedule you created by trying to end their nighttime visits.

Just make sure you gently explain to them the reasons why they need to stay and sleep in their bedroom the entire night. Implementing this sleep schedule without fail for a couple of weeks will surely help your child sleep independently without requiring the help of anyone, including you.

- *Not making gradual adjustments* - Remember that it will take a bit of time for your child to get used to the new sleeping routines and schedule. It is the reason why you must avoid expecting them to adjust right away. Do not make the mistake of rushing the process.

You have to let them adjust slowly. Understand that changing their sleep schedule overnight is impossible, so making minor and small changes gradually is what you must do. Make adjustments—for instance, through fifteen-minute increments—to the bedtime schedule until the specific bedtime you want your child to follow is reached.

Avoid these seven mistakes, and you will surely have a high chance of making your toddler stick to the bedtime or sleep schedule you already set up. Again, be consistent and firm when trying to make them follow the routines and new sleep schedule.

Running these similar activities every night sends messages and cues to their brain that it is already time for them to sleep. By establishing calming pre-bed routines and setting up an appropriate sleep schedule, your toddler will be able to wind down, promoting better sleep for them as well as a lower risk of having middle of the night awakenings.

Chapter 10: The Growing Toddler: Dealing with Change

One thing you should remember about toddlers and children is they tend to grow fast. This means their sleeping habits will also most likely change in the future. How can you help your growing toddler deal with the changes they will most likely encounter during their growth and development?

How can you help them adjust to various sleeping patterns and the transitions they need to make? The last chapter of this book aims to find answers to your questions so that you can guide your child toward dealing with all the changes that they may find confusing and alarming. It is especially true if the change involves getting separated from their parents as they transition into a bigger bed and a new bedroom.

Making Adjustments on Various Sleeping Routines and Habits

Depending on your toddler's or child's age, they may need to make constant adjustments to sleeping routines and habits. There is no need to make a drastic change. It would be best to make gradual changes—something your child will not notice right away to prevent the drama and other unnecessary and unwanted reactions.

Make sure you make adjustments to your growing child's routines based on their age and the specific amount of sleep they need at that particular time. For instance, at around six months old, they need to meet the daily required number of sleep hours, which is around ten to eleven hours.

Here, you have to incorporate two to three naps during the daytime, with the first two naps being around one and a half to two hours each. Train your child to have a shorter nap. Once they reach around nine months, expect them to need around ten to twelve hours of shut-eye. One of the major adjustments you have to make during this time is the elimination of night feeding.

You have to focus on completely weaning them and feeding solid foods, so they will no longer ask for night feeds. At this age, two naps—taking about one and a half to two hours each—during the daytime will be okay. Make sure not to set naptimes before 3:30 to 4:30 in the afternoon.

Ensure you introduce the habit of napping after lunch so that they will wake up by 3:00 p.m. That way, you can give them enough activities right after their nap, which will use all their energy and make them fully prepared for bed by around 7:00 to 9:00 in the evening.

You have to try introducing good sleeping habits, even just minor ones, to your child before they hit one-year-old. That way, making major adjustments regarding their sleep will be much easier moving forward.

Remember that once they get into toddlerhood, instilling new habits and routines will be much more challenging. This is because they will most likely resist new changes, so training them to follow even just minor bedtime routines before that can help.

One- to Two-year-old Routines

Upon reaching one year old, expect your child to be more active. They will also become more resistant and most likely want to do things their way, making it a bit harder to let them adjust to the changes in their sleep. During this age, one reminder is to make sure that they constantly receive around ten to twelve hours of sleep, including two naps with a duration of one to two hours each.

At one and a half years, they will need around eleven to twelve hours of sleep every night. It is also the time when you and your toddler will have to adjust naptimes because it will drop to just one during the day. To make it easier to stick to, set this one nap around lunchtime, allowing it to take around one and a half to two hours.

As for bedtime, make sure you set a consistent schedule for them to sleep and wake up. That way, they will not have a hard time adjusting to the routines. Note that your child can smoothly survive any major change in bedtime and sleeping routines if you set a regular bedtime.

Also, try to make bedtimes predictable. Help them sleep on time by preventing them from doing fun and exciting stuff that might only further raise their energy, like outdoor play. It would help if you also stopped feeding them with sugary snacks, drinks, and meals thirty minutes or so before bedtime.

It also helps if their dinner consists of foods containing carbs, like cereals or rice and bread. Let them drink milk at dinnertime too. Such foods can stimulate the production of melatonin, a hormone necessary for sleep. If you already give your child a little screen time, do not set it up close to bedtime.

This means turning off the TV, other gadgets, and screens one hour or so before their bedtime. You can further make them accustomed to bedtime by doing the following during that period:

- Brushing their teeth
- Changing into a new and clean diaper
- Turning their night light on – It can prevent them from feeling extremely upset if they wake up and realize they are all alone in the dark. Make sure to stay away from blue lights, and choose red and yellow night-lights.
- Tucking them into bed while they are still awake but already drowsy
- Letting them relax by reading a short story

With all these routines set, adjusting to new sleeping habits based on their age will be manageable.

Transitioning to a New and Big Bed

Some parents agree that the best time to start letting their kids transition to a newer and bigger bed is between one to two years old. You can also do the same for your child, but be prepared to make them feel safe and secure, even if you are no longer sharing the same bed or bedroom. Expect resistance during the transition since this is a huge change your child has to go through, but you can manage such a challenge with these simple tips:

Determine if They are Ready First

It is hard to resist the temptation of making your toddler move to a new bed and room as soon as they hit around one or two. However, avoid doing it right away without scrutinizing your child's readiness level because not all toddlers are ready to take the leap even when they reach such an age.

There are even those who only seem to be ready when they get close to three years old or so. It is mainly because toddlers are strongly attached to you, their crib, and their sleep associations. Those things make them feel safe and secure when it is time to go to bed. With those considerations in mind, avoid rushing the process.

The perfect time to transition them to a new bedroom is when you start noticing them asking for it. If possible, wait for them to show signs that they are ready before taking the big leap. You may also want to discuss it with them slowly. Explain how good it will be for them to have their own bed and room where they will have freedom and independence. Make sure your toddler never thinks of their bedroom as an area of punishment because this negative connection will disrupt your attempts to teach your toddler to go to bed peacefully in their room. If you need a timeout area, keep it away from the bedroom so that it will be a safe place for the child psychologically.

Pick the Right Toddler Bed

Make sure you are also very cautious when it comes to choosing your child's bed. They are sure to feel excited to transition if they see how great their toddler bed is. In this case, you have a couple of options—including a toddler bed resembling a smaller version of a twin bed.

You can go for one that comes in the form of a fire truck, princess castle, or race car. Your goal is to look for a concept and style your toddler will surely love, thereby enticing them to move to it.

Another choice is a twin bed with safety rails outfitted. The two are great options, so you can pick one based on your budget, the amount of space in your child's bedroom, and their temperament. Go for a sturdy and durable bed too. Remember that it is for a child that will most likely roll, jump, bounce, wiggle, and do other fun and exciting stuff.

You need to look for a bed capable of withstanding the daily use and abuse of most toddlers. Make sure the bed is low to the ground and has safety rails. It is necessary to prevent your child from getting injured due to falling accidentally. They can also easily get in and out of the toddler bed if it is low to the ground.

Allow Your Child to Participate in the Process

This means you should get them involved in the transition. For instance, you can make them choose the design for their toddler bed, so you can provoke their excitement and further encourage them to move into their new room. Allow them to choose the bedding and sheets too. You should also encourage them to customize their new room and bed. If you have a limited budget, just give them alternatives you can afford.

Customizing the room can be achieved by arranging their favorite toys and stuffed animals based on what they want. Whether you decide to go for a twin or toddler bed, make it a point to let your toddler participate during the selection process.

Reinforce New Bedtime Rules

If you have made your toddler agree to sleep in a new room or bed, it is highly likely they will love their newfound freedom and independence. This may make it hard for them to resist exploring and roaming around their new environment. It is not a good idea, though, especially if they tend to explore very close to bedtime.

With that in mind, you have to reinforce new bedtime rules to minimize their need to explore. One rule you may want to set in place is to schedule a last call or request for their favorite toy, water, or a trip to the bathroom before you finally tuck them into bed. Be firm and make them understand how important it is to follow the new rules.

Childproof the Home

When your child has to transition to a new bed and room, you have to begin reevaluating the childproofing methods you have set in place. Before making the transfer, find out if you need to set other safety measures and precautions in place that will guarantee your toddler's safety in case they end up adventuring at night.

One tip is to use safety gates to block all stairwells. Make it a point to lock the windows and all doors leading outdoors. Moreover, you have to make sure they cannot reach those areas where you keep harmful materials as well as certain medications and cleaning products. You can also have covers put on electrical outlets.

Childproofing your home, not just your toddler's bedroom, is especially important, especially if they are someone who loves to roam around and explore. It is all the more important if they tend to sleepwalk, making them more prone to getting injured.

Put Their New Stuff in the Proper Places

Note that being consistent is extremely necessary when trying to introduce new changes. The same is true when you are working with toddlers. With that in mind, you need to position their bed and other important stuff in their bedroom appropriately. As much as possible, position the new toddler bed at the same spot as their crib used to be.

Keep in mind that some toddlers get too stressed when they notice you moving everything related to them, so try to be consistent. You should also try to arrange and decorate their room similar to what they were used to. Observe your child's personality, as this will help you judge the best way to make the transition and position their stuff.

Empathize

One more thing you have to do as a parent is to empathize with your child. Take into account that every change is difficult. Even adults have a hard time accepting a sudden change, so expect your toddler to be stressed and pressured throughout the process. They may get too clingy, cry incessantly, or resist during the adjustment. You can handle that by showing empathy.

Let them know how much you understand how they feel and how difficult the transition is for them. You can also relay what you felt when you were their age and finally moved to a new bed. Your goal is to make them understand that someone understands their situation. Also, reassure them that you will always be around to guide them as they make the adjustments. That way, they will not feel too frightened of the new changes.

Dealing with Sudden Changes in a Preschooler's Sleep Schedule

Another major adjustment your child will have to go through is when they become of school age. They may feel extremely excited about this milestone, but it could also mean sudden changes in their sleep schedule that will greatly affect their lifestyle.

For instance, naptimes may get affected. Most kids around the ages of three to five require around eleven to thirteen hours of sleep each night. Also, most of these preschoolers have set naptimes during the day. These naps often range from one to two hours. You can expect these kids to stop napping upon reaching five.

You have to remember that each preschooler is different. While some stick to the nap routines they get used to, others refuse to nap once they become a preschooler. If your child is one who refuses a nap, you do not have to fret.

The technique here is to remain calm and consistent. Moreover, set a goal to make them get a minimum of eleven hours of sleep every night. That way, you do not have to worry too much if they ditch the nap during the daytime. Just make sure you also replace this ditched nap with quiet time or downtime involving relaxing activities, such as reading.

Another thing to keep in mind is that once your child gets into preschool, they may feel extremely tired once they come home. It is because of school activities and routines, especially if they have just started taking part in them. With that said, you should try to make adjustments to their routines, particularly those involving their sleep.

That way, they will restore lost energy and wake up feeling refreshed to take on the day. The following tips will make it easier for your child to adjust to their new life as a preschooler:

• *Set a regular bedtime* – Try to avoid putting them to bed too early, though. Your goal is to make them get into the habit of falling asleep thirty minutes after you put them to bed. Once they start preschool, you may want to schedule their bedtime a bit later so that they may achieve that. You can set it at 8:00 or 9:00 in the evening to make it a lot easier for them to settle down.

• *Establish limitations and boundaries during bedtime* – For instance, if you already told them you would read them only one story, make sure you follow through with that. Never give in; otherwise, you will have a harder time training them.

• *Set aside a relaxing and quiet time before their sleep schedule* – Your goal here is to help your child calm down and relax before bedtime. Try to set aside a quiet time with them that takes around thirty to 45 minutes. Activities you can incorporate here are storytelling, quiet play, coloring, jigsaw puzzles, dressing up for bed, turning off the light, and staying away from screens and TV an hour or so before bedtime.

- *Give rewards* – One of the most effective ways to reinforce a new habit and make your child adjust to new routines is to offer rewards. If they successfully stay in their bed and sleep on time, then you can reward them. This will motivate them to stick to the habits, promoting faster adjustments.

Sleep training can be extremely challenging, especially if your child needs to face a major change that will require them to make a sudden and huge adjustment to their usual routines. You can help them by letting them know you will always be there for them.

Remember that one of the secrets to managing any transition and a major change in your child's sleeping habits and routines is your patience. Be patient and prepare yourself for resistance on their part.

Handle your child calmly and constantly reassure them that you are still around, even if they are already in a new room and bed. Eventually, they will get used to the routines and make the necessary adjustments.

Conclusion

Now that you have finished reading this book, you are armed with all the information required for successful toddler sleep training. Use all the mentioned tips as your guide, and you will certainly eliminate most, if not all, of the problems that might stop your toddler from getting their much-needed rest.

You can tweak the tips a bit based on your unique situation and your child's distinctive personality and behaviors. Note that you cannot expect all children to be the same, so their responses may also be different. With that said, pick those tips, strategies, and tricks guaranteed to help your child finally have better quality and sound sleep.

Moreover, you will be thankful if you are successful with sleep training because it will also mean longer and better sleep for you and your family.

Here's another book by Meryl Kaufman that you might like

References

https://www.youtube.com/watch?v=gRZD0Y01xmI

https://www.italiansrus.com/articles/whoami6.htm

https://amshq.org/About-Montessori/History-of-Montessori/Who-Was-Maria-Montessori

https://www.livingmontessori.com/montessori-method/history-of-the-montessori-method/

https://www.montessori.edu/FAQ.html

https://www.public-montessori.org/montessori/.

https://www.montessorieducation.com/blog/alexander-graham-bell-and-montessori

https://www.bartleby.com/essay/Describe-in-Detail-the-Three-Elements-of-FKDK6CS5H3U4Z1.

https://amshq.org/About-Montessori/What-Is-Montessori/Terminology

https://www.retrogamer.net/retro_games90/the-making-of-the-sims/

https://www.newamerica.org/weekly/bezos-montessori-education/

https://www.montessorieducation.com/blog/jeff-bezos-amazon-just-gave-1-billion-to-montessori-inspired-preschools-now-what-is-montessori

https://www.edweek.org/ew/articles/2018/09/26/the-montessori-mafia-why-tech-titans-like.html

https://indianamontessoriacademy.org/eight-principles-of-montessori-education/https://indianamontessoriacademy.org/eight-principles-of-montessori-education/

https://montessori-nw.org/about-montessori-education

http://psychosocialdisney.blogspot.com/2015/07/well-begun-is-half-done.html

https://www.youtube.com/watch?v=GhANk9tIW9s

https://montessoriacademy.com.au/montessori-education/montessori-principles-education/

http://forestmontessori.com/brain-development-from-birth-to-three-years/

https://www.kidcentraltn.com/development/1-3-years/brain-development-toddlers-1-3-years.html

http://images.pcmac.org/SiSFiles/Schools/CA/SMJUHSD/PioneerValleyHigh/Uploads/DocumentsSubCategories/Documents/Chapter08_WHYL-A.pdf

https://nancyguberti.com/5-stages-of-human-brain-development/

https://www.youtube.com/watch?v=XmMhQD84_1E

https://theeducatorsroom.com/being-a-parent-and-a-teacher-an-impossible-combination/

https://www.psychologicalscience.org/observer/perception-and-play-how-children-view-the-world

https://www.youtube.com/watch?v=DZUhxuKyucM

https://www.youtube.com/watch?v=ypR-P1gAfas

https://www.montessoriprintshop.com/observation.html

https://www.youtube.com/watch?v=xVHJlIch5nk

https://www.youtube.com/watch?v=YaCbwVARh5I

https://www.youtube.com/watch?v=pp7iH4qhPtM

https://www.montessoriteachered.com/the-montessori-muse-blog/2018/8/15/a-montessori-manor-how-to-help-parents-incorporate-a-montessori-mindset-at-home

https://www.healthlinkbc.ca/health-topics/ue5465

https://www.goodstart.org.au/news-and-advice/october-2016/exploring-the-benefits-of-sensory-play

https://www.youtube.com/watch?v=_wq3jpl7GUc

https://www.youtube.com/watch?v=PC6vKh3bhTI

https://www.themontessorinotebook.com/age-appropriate-chores-for-children/

https://www.mother.ly/child/montessori-ways-your-toddler-can-help-around-the-house

https://www.youtube.com/watch?v=WT5ViWO24xk

https://voilamontessori.com/montessori-children-and-chores/

https://www.youtube.com/watch?v=4Uyzls0Xs0U

https://www.azquotes.com/quote/1206104

https://nafme.org/music-education-montessori-lens-every-child-musical-potential/

https://www.montessoriservices.com/ideas-insights/music-in-the-montessori-classroo

https://www.montessoriservices.com/music-movement/instruments

https://www.themontessorinotebook.com/montessori-and-music/

https://livingmontessorinow.com/montessori-inspired-music-activities-for-toddlers-and-preschoolers/

http://www.montessori-blog.org/2018/05/16/famous-people-who-attended-montessori-beyonce-knowles/

https://www.youtube.com/watch?v=YvybLbW_D5Q

https://momtessorilife.com/2015/09/04/language-photo-cards-family/

https://www.youtube.com/watch?v=vmqen3cueuY

https://livingmontessorinow.com/learning-to-read-can-be-just-a-fun-game/

https://guidepostmontessori.com/blog/teaching-reading-writing-montessori

https://www.youtube.com/watch?v=Qq90WOn3xAY

https://www.everystarisdifferent.com/2016/01/learning-montessori-way-writing.html

https://blog.workman.com/2019/04/montessori-method-encourage-creativity-child/

https://thomaspark.co/2015/11/bob-ross-color-palette-in-css/

https://www.howwemontessori.com/how-we-montessori/crafts/

https://mymodernmet.com/pointillism-art-georges-seurat/

https://www.iheartnaptime.net/play-dough-recipe/

https://www.instructables.com/id/How-to-use-spaghetti-to-paint-like-Jackson-Pollock/

https://blog.hubspot.com/sales/self-discipline

http://ageofmontessori.org/teach-children-self-discipline-instead-obedience/

https://www.youtube.com/watch?v=SckUevGH-Pk

https://www.livingmontessori.com/positive-discipline-and-child-guidance/

https://www.youtube.com/watch?v=nt9ck98l8Uo

https://www.howwemontessori.com/how-we-montessori/2011/08/my-baby-is-teething.html

https://www.montessoridowntown.com/handle-a-clingy-toddler/

https://www.youtube.com/watch?v=iL_vvFAH8AY

https://www.themontessorinotebook.com/stop-tantrum-yes-read-right/

https://www.familyeducation.com/life/communicating-your-toddler/how-have-conversation-your-three-year-old

https://www.happiestbaby.com/blogs/toddler/teaching-patience-toddlers